THE LITTLE BOOK OF BATH

MIKE DEAN

Mike Dean.

The
History
Press

First published 2017

The History Press
The Mill, Brimscombe Port
Stroud, Gloucestershire, GL5 2QG
www.thehistorypress.co.uk

British Library Cataloguing in Publication Data.
A catalogue record for this book is available from the British Library.

ISBN 978 0 7509 6603 0

Typesetting and origination by The History Press
Printed and bound in Great Britain by TJ International Ltd.

CONTENTS

ACKNOWLEDGEMENTS

The writing of this book would not have been possible without the help of numerous people. In particular, I would like to express my thanks to some of my friends and colleagues in Bath Parade Guides for their interest and for allowing me to access their considerable store of collective knowledge. Thanks also to Colin Johnston, Principal Archivist at Bath Record Office, and the staff for their skill and patience, to Graham Champken and Mick Butler for their help and advice with illustrations and to Nicola Guy and Beth Amphlett at The History Press for encouraging me to write this book. Also to my wife, Gwyneth, for her input in the form of support, ideas and suggestions. To all these, and others, I offer my gratitude. Any errors or omissions are entirely my responsibility.

ABOUT THE AUTHOR

Mike Dean is a retired primary school teacher and a registered 'Blue Badge' Tour Guide for the West of England. A graduate of Bristol University, his hobbies include reading, walking, music and travel. He is passionately interested in sailing ships and in the folklore of the West Country. This is his first book.

INTRODUCTION

Visitors to Bath come for all kinds of reasons – the Georgian architecture, the Roman Baths, the cultural and historical associations, the shopping, to name just a few. Whatever their reasons, however, Bath rarely fails to captivate, as the city has something for everyone. Over its 2,000 years of existence it has seen and experienced a great deal, and the evidence of its history is still there to be enjoyed by those who are prepared to look. Even those who think they know Bath well can make unexpected discoveries around the next corner or pick up some nugget of new information.

For example:

The Orange Grove, behind Bath Abbey, has nothing to do with the fruit. It was named because of the visit in 1734 of William, Prince of the Dutch House of Orange, who came to Bath to take the 'water cure'.

As well as its grand Georgian architecture, Bath has its share of brutalist buildings, such as Manvers Street Police Station (1962), the Hilton Hotel (1973) and the Bus Station (2009), which has famously been compared to a baked bean tin.

On a visit to Bath in 1794, the great composer Joseph Haydn wrote a canon in honour of Turk, a dog who belonged to Venanzio Rauzzini, the Director of Music in the city at the time.

Bath is the possessor of the only hot geothermal springs in Britain, with a temperature of more than 40°C. To qualify as a 'hot' spring, the water must be above body temperature (36.9°C).

The city has its own local currency, known as the 'Bath Oliver', which takes the form of a voucher that can be exchanged for local goods and services. There has been a suggestion that it should be replaced with a 'Bath Pound' (like the 'Bristol Pound' used by Bath's neighbouring city).

More than 12,000 votive offerings, thrown there in Roman times, have been recovered from the Sacred Spring in the Roman Baths. Many are on display in the Baths Museum. There are also more than a hundred 'curse tablets', inscribed on lead and dating from the second to the fourth centuries AD, almost all of which are asking for retribution against wrongdoers.

This book does not lay claim to be a history of Bath, nor to be exhaustive or definitive, and anyone who wishes to delve more deeply into the background of this fascinating city is encouraged to consult some of the many excellent and well-researched volumes that have been produced over the years. What I have attempted to do here is to compile a collection of interesting, unusual (and in some cases, bizarre) information which I hope will prove of interest to the reader, whether a visitor or someone who is already familiar with Bath. Any collection such as this must inevitably be subjective, and cannot cover everything, so if I have not included a particular favourite of yours, I can only apologise, and would be happy to hear from you. All the information is, to the best of my knowledge, accurate at the time of writing.

1

SOME FACTS AND FIGURES

WHERE IS BATH?

Bath stands at Latitude N 51° 23′, W 02° 22′, and at its centre is 192ft (58.5m) above sea level. The major cities in the world with the closest co-ordinates to Bath are Bristol, England, and Leipzig, Germany. Bath's population is currently (2017) around 89,000, and it lies within the unitary authority of Bath and North East Somerset (B&NES), in the historic county of Somerset. It stands near the southern edge of the Cotswolds in the valley of the river Avon and covers an area of about 11 square miles (approx. 28.5 sq. km.)

It has formal status as a city, and has a mayor who is chosen annually by the elected councillors. Bath is one of the oldest parliamentary constituencies in the country, having existed since 1295, and sends one member to Parliament.

Bath's principal industry is heritage and cultural tourism, and in 1987 it was designated a World Heritage Site by UNESCO. The city welcomes almost 4 million day-visitors per year, and over 1 million who stay for longer. Other major employers include the National Health Service, B&NES Council and the two universities, Bath and Bath Spa. Bath has more than 400 retail shops and several theatres. Its local newspaper is the *Bath Chronicle*, published weekly.

BY ANY OTHER NAME

During its long history Bath has been known by a variety of names. The Romans called it Aquae Sulis (the 'Waters of Sulis') after the deity who was regarded as the guardian of the springs by the Celtic Dobunni tribe who occupied the area before the Romans came. It was also sometimes known by the name of Aquae Calidae ('Hot Waters').

During Saxon times there were several names: Akemanceaster (which may derive from the 'aquae' part of Bath's Roman name; the Roman road named Akeman Street ran nearby and may originally have linked with Bath). Later in the Saxon period the name was changed to Bathanceaster and then to Hat Batha (or Bathum).

Bath is also a serious candidate for being the 'Badon' or 'Caer Badon' where the semi-mythical King Arthur is said to have fought his most famous battle, in which he defeated the Saxons. In his *Historia Brittonum* (*c.* 830) the Welsh monk Nennius mentions 'the Baths of Badon'.

The sixteenth/seventeenth-century writer and topographer William Camden (1551–1623), in his great work *Britannia*, the first systematic survey of Great Britain and Ireland, quotes several historical names for Bath, including Badiza, Bathonia, Yr Ennaint Twymin ('the city in the warm vale') and Caer Palladur ('the City of Pallas'). 'Pallas' was a name, or title, sometimes given to the goddess Athena, who is, of course, the Greek equivalent of the Roman goddess Minerva, firmly linked to Bath.

THE POPULATION OF BATH

The following figures are approximate, but indicate how Bath's population has grown over the centuries:

1300	800
1400	1,000
1500	1,200

1600	2,000
1700	3,000
1800	32,000
1900	65,000
2000	83,000
2011	88,000

TOWNS THAT ARE TWINNED WITH BATH

Aix-en-Provence: A city-commune in the south of France, about 19 miles (30km) north of Marseilles. It has its own springs and the Romans called it 'Aquae Sextiae'. The fact that it is also a spa town led to its twinning with Bath.

Alkmaar: A city in the province of north Holland, it is well-known for its traditional cheese market. John Lennon's first guitar was made here and there is a museum to The Beatles. The twinning connection came about because the citizens of Bath held fundraising events to support the people of Alkmaar who had suffered during the German occupation.

Braunschweig (Brunswick): A city in Lower Saxony, Germany, it is a major centre for scientific research and development. The link between the two cities was established shortly after the Second World War as part of a government initiative designed to bring together young people from England and Germany.

Kaposvár: A city in south western Hungary, its name means 'castle of gates'. Thermal waters were discovered here in the 1960s and the two cities were twinned in 1989.

Beppu: A city in the Ōita Prefecture on the island of Kyushu, Japan, like Bath, it is famous for its hot springs ('*onsen*' in Japanese).

Bath also has a historic partnership agreement with Manly, a seaside suburb of Sydney, Australia. It was given its name by (then) Captain Arthur Phillip, first Governor of New South Wales, who declared that the 'confidence and manly bearing' of the local population led to his naming the place Manly Cove.

In addition, the suburbs of Batheaston and Bathford are twinned with Oudun and Artannes-sur-Indre (both in France) respectively.

PLACES IN THE USA NAMED AFTER BATH

Bath, California
Bath, Illinois
Bath, Indiana
Bath, Maine
Bath, Michigan
Bath, New Hampshire
Bath, New York State
Bath, North Carolina
Bath, Pennsylvania
Bath, South Carolina
Bath, South Dakota
Bath, West Virginia

Bath County, Kentucky
Bath County, Virginia

THE SEVEN HILLS OF BATH

Rome is built on seven hills; Bath is surrounded by seven hills. They are:

1. Beechen Cliff, with its heavily wooded slopes, provides a dramatic backdrop to the view to the south of the city. Immortalised by Jane Austen in *Northanger Abbey* as the place

where Catherine Morland takes her walk with Tilneys, it gives superb views over the city and is part of Bath's Skyline Walk.

2. Southdown has much interwar and post-war development. The area is dominated by High Barrow Hill (known locally as Round Hill), which has been kept as an open recreational area.

3. Lansdown (meaning 'the long hill') lies to the north east. In 1643 the Battle of Lansdown, between Royalist and Parliamentarian forces, was fought here, and there is a monument to the Royalist commander Sir Bevil Grenville. Today the area has football fields and a famous racecourse.

4. Kelston Round Hill to the west of the city, crowned with trees, is a landmark which can be seen for miles around. It is also known locally as 'Kelston Tump' ('tump' is an old dialect word meaning a small rounded hill or mound).

5. Solsbury Hill (or Little Solsbury Hill, as it is sometimes known) is small, flat-topped and the site of an Iron Age hillfort. At 625ft (191m) it stands above the village of Batheaston. It inspired the song 'Solsbury Hill', written by rock musician Peter Gabriel and recorded in 1977 as his first solo single.

6. Bathampton Down is a flat limestone plateau that overlooks the city from the north west. It has evidence of human occupation dating back to prehistoric times. On its southern slopes is Claverton Manor, an 1820s mansion that is now the home of the American Museum in Britain.

7. Bathford Hill lies to the east and there was once an ancient ford close by. In the days of horse-drawn traffic, extra horses, needed to pull carriages up the hill, were kept in a nearby field.

LONGEST, SHORTEST, OLDEST, TALLEST …

Bath's widest street is Great Pulteney Street, at 100ft (30m). It is also the longest, at 1,100ft (335m). (Broad Street, which sounds as if it ought to be one of the widest, is in fact quite narrow. It takes its name from the broadcloth that used to be woven there.) The shortest street in the city is Sunderland Street, at only 75ft (23m) long.

The narrowest alley in the city can be found in Northgate Street, near to the Podium Shopping Centre. This was the medieval Alford Lane, otherwise known as 'Slippery Lane'. Bath's widest pavement is the pedestrianised Duke Street, with a width of 50ft (15m) between the houses.

The tallest church spire is that of St John the Evangelist in South Parade, at 222ft (68m).

For many years it was thought that the oldest surviving house in Bath was Sally Lunn's in North Parade Passage; in fact a plaque on the outside proclaims this, giving a date of 1482. However, in 2000, renovations to Nos 21 and 22 High Street revealed details of a late medieval wattle-and-daub construction that is almost certainly older.

The oldest bridge in Bath is (oddly enough) New Bridge, which dates from 1734. It carries the A4 Bristol road across the river Avon to the west of Bath.

Bath's most expensive building to date is the Thermae Bath Spa, opened in August 2006 at a cost of around £45 million. The original estimate in 1996 had been £13 million! However, it has been a huge success and contributes over £15 million a year to Bath's economy.

Bath's largest park is the Royal Victoria Park on the west side of the city. It covers an area of some 57 acres (23 hectares).

Bath's oldest public house is probably the Coeur de Lion in Northumberland Place (see p.138).

Bath's deepest canal lock is located on the Kennet and Avon Canal at Widcombe. At 19ft 5in (5.92m) deep it is the second deepest lock on the British waterways system. Bath Deep Lock, as it is called, was formed when two locks were combined in 1976.

Britain's longest cycling tunnel is located in Bath. Combe Down Tunnel, part of the Two Tunnels Greenway route, is 1,829 yards (1.7km) in length.

SOME POPULAR MISCONCEPTIONS ABOUT BATH

Here are some common 'facts' about Bath, which are not true:

Bath lies in the County of Avon. In fact, County Avon no longer exists. It was created as the result of administrative changes to county boundaries in 1974, but was abolished in 1996, to the satisfaction of many local people. The city is now part of the unitary authority of Bath and North East Somerset.

Jane Austen loved Bath. Although two of her novels, *Persuasion* and *Northanger Abbey*, are largely set in Bath, and the city gets a mention in most of her others, Jane was not over-fond of the place, as some of her letters show. In a letter of 1808, she declares: 'It will be two years tomorrow since we left Bath for Clifton, with what happy feelings of escape'. These feelings might perhaps be partly explained by her aunt's arrest and subsequent trial in 1799 on a false charge of shoplifting.

A 'Sally Lunn' is another name for the Bath Bun. They are, in fact, two different things. The Bath Bun (sometimes known as a 'London Bath Bun') is a round, rich bun with a topping of sugar crystals and a lump of sugar baked into its base. The Sally Lunn is larger, light and spongy like a French brioche, and usually eaten with a sweet or savoury topping. The authentic version is made exclusively at Sally Lunn's Historic Eating House in Bath, to a recipe said to date from the seventeenth century.

Some of Bath's elegant buildings were designed by Beau Nash. Richard 'Beau' Nash (1674–1761) was Bath's famous eighteenth-century Master of the Ceremonies and the arbiter of taste, fashion and behaviour in the city. Visitors sometimes confuse him with John Nash (1752–1835), the architect responsible for much of the layout of Regency London, as well as such innovative schemes as Blaise Hamlet in Bristol and the Royal Pavilion, Brighton.

'Shakespeare's Avon' runs through Bath on its way to the sea. The river that runs through Bath is indeed the Avon, but not the one associated with the great playwright. That's the Warwickshire Avon; ours is the Gloucestershire Avon. There are actually five rivers named 'Avon' in England, three in Scotland and one in Wales. Canada and New Zealand each have two, while Australia has five. 'Avon' (or '*afon*') is simply an old Celtic word meaning 'river'.

One of Bath's Masters of Ceremonies was Beau Brummell. Richard 'Beau' Nash is sometimes confused with the Regency dandy George Bryan 'Beau' Brummell (1778–1840), arbiter of male fashion and a great friend (for a while) of the Prince Regent, the future George IV. No record seems to exist of a visit to Bath by Brummell, but it is known that he favoured 'Bath coating' for his tailcoat. This was a thick, double-raised heavy woollen cloth with a long nap, produced in the city.

The film *Oliver!* was partly shot in Bath. Many people think that the famous scene in the film version of Lionel Bart's musical *Oliver!* (1968), where the young Twist looks out of the window to see the street vendors parading their wares and singing 'Who Will Buy?', was filmed in the Royal Crescent. In fact, the location was just a large and elaborate film set at Shepperton Studios in Surrey.

Bath Abbey is a cathedral. Despite its impressive size and style, the abbey is not a cathedral – in fact, technically it is no longer even an abbey! During the Middle Ages, the abbey had been part a Benedictine monastery. When Bishop John of Tours decided to establish his seat (or 'cathedra') here around 1088, the building became a cathedral priory. However, later bishops preferred to live at Wells, which then became the cathedral for the diocese (Bath and Wells), as it is today. With the Dissolution in 1539 the building became a parish church, and so it remains. Nonetheless, it is still known traditionally as 'Bath Abbey'.

The abbey's flying buttresses are 'fakes'. Visitors have, not infrequently, been heard to declare this. Originally, the abbey did not have flying buttresses because the nave only had a flat roof, so they were not needed. In an attempt to improve the look of the building, flying buttresses were added in the 1830s, but were only of light construction as they did not need to counteract any thrust. Thirty years later, stone fan vaulting was added to the nave, but the buttresses were not strengthened, and in a few years the walls were being pushed apart. New, solid buttresses were added in order to solve the problem. So, yes – they are genuine!

IT HAPPENED FIRST IN BATH

Here are a few of the things that first occurred in Bath:

In 1781, while studying the stars through his home-made telescope in the garden of his house in New King Street, William (later Sir William) Herschel discovered the planet now known as Uranus, along with two of its moons. The following year he was appointed the King's Astronomer to George III. Herschel was also a noted organist and composer.

Workmen digging a trench in Stall Street in 1717 unearthed a bronze gilded head representing the Roman goddess Minerva. She was the goddess of wisdom and military success and the head is thought to have come from a statue in the Temple of Sulis Minerva, which once stood nearby. The head can be seen in the Roman Baths Museum.

During an archaeological survey in 2012 on the site of the new Gainsborough Hotel, a hoard of more than 17,500 Roman silver coins, some as old as 32 BC, was discovered. The coins were contained in eight leather bags and are believed to be the largest hoard from a Roman settlement ever found in Britain. They have been valued by the Treasury Valuations Committee at £120,000, and the Roman Baths Museum has raised £60,000 to be able to acquire and display them.

In the year 973 King Edgar was crowned in the then Bath Abbey, a forerunner of the present building. According to some definitions, he was the first King of all England. The form of service devised for that occasion is, essentially, the same as the one used for Coronation services today. A stained-glass window in the east end of the abbey commemorates this event.

John Wood the Elder's Circus, begun in 1754, is the first example in the country of a street built in a circular form. The columns on the façades of the thirty-three houses show the three principal orders of Classical architecture: Doric (flat tops), Ionic (curly tops) and Corinthian (leafy tops).

Bath was the first city outside London to have an electricity company. The City of Bath Electric Light and Engineering Co. Ltd was formed in 1890 to supply 'electric force' and to maintain 'appliances now known or to be invented'.

On 11 December 1799 William Smith, then living at No. 22 Great Pulteney Street, first dictated his list of the geological strata that lay beneath the English countryside – a breakthrough in the study of geology. In 1815 he produced 'The Map That Changed the World': the first geological map of Britain. He became known as 'Strata' Smith, and is regarded as the father of English geology.

The world's first postage stamp (Rowland Hill's famous 'Penny Black') was issued in Bath on 2 May 1840, four days before it was scheduled to be officially launched. This is believed to be due to an error on the part of a rather over-enthusiastic postmistress.

Plasticine was invented in Bath by art teacher William Harbutt in 1897. He needed a non-drying, clay-like modelling medium for use by his sculpture students. It became popular worldwide, and has been extensively used in the film animation industry. Plasticine continued to be manufactured in the Bathampton factory until 1983, when the factory closed and production was moved to Thailand. The brand has since passed through a succession of owners. Today it is produced by GP Flair PLC, a company based in Cheam, Surrey, which holds the rights to its manufacture.

In the summer of 1897 the 22-year-old Winston Churchill made his first political speech from the steps of Claverton Manor. It took place during a fete that had been arranged by the Bath Conservative Association.

In the 1590s Sir John Harington, a godson to Elizabeth I, invented the first example of a flushing toilet, which he installed in his manor at Kelston, near Bath. The term 'john', when used (particularly in the USA) to refer to a toilet, is sometimes regarded as a direct reference to its inventor.

WHAT'S IN A NAME?

A number of products have been named after the city of Bath, usually because of their association with it. Here are some:

The Bath Bun (not to be confused with the Sally Lunn): This is a rich, round bun with a lump of sugar baked into its base, and sugar crystals and currants or caraway seeds sprinkled on the top. It probably originated in the eighteenth century and acquired the nickname of the 'London' Bath Bun when nearly a million of them were eaten there during the Great Exhibition of 1851.

The Bath Chap: This is the lower half of a pig's cheek, salted or pickled in brine then smoked, boiled and finally coated in breadcrumbs. It is a local delicacy.

The Bath Chair: This was the successor to the sedan chair. It is a type of wheelchair with a folding hood, which can be pushed or pulled by an attendant or steered by the occupant.

Bath Blue: This is a classic blue-veined organic cheese made by the Bath Soft Cheese Company at Kelston, near Bath.

Bath Stone: Used almost exclusively in the building of the city, this is an oolitic limestone that was quarried or mined from the hills surrounding Bath. Today, the nearest working quarries are at Corsham, Wiltshire.

The Bath Oliver: This is a plain, hard biscuit invented in the eighteenth century by Dr William Oliver, physician at the Mineral Water Hospital. It was an early form of health food for his patients, although you can now buy them covered in rich, dark chocolate.

The Beauty of Bath: A small green apple flushed with red, this was introduced into the area in 1864. They are not often found in shops, as they must be eaten soon after picking or they will rot.

Bath Ales: This is an independent local brewery, established in 1995, which produces a range of craft beers and ciders. It is actually located in Warmley, a few miles north-west of Bath.

Bath Aqua Glass: This takes its name from the Roman name for the city, Aquae Sulis, and is made by adding copper oxide to the molten glass, giving it its distinctive aquamarine colour. It is handmade in the city.

Bath Asparagus: This is the common name for *ornithogalum pyrenaicum*, a plant whose flower shoots can be eaten as a vegetable. It takes its name from the fact that it was once found in abundance near the city. Among its other names are 'spiked star of Bethlehem' and 'poor man's asparagus' from the fact that it once formed part of the diet of the poorer folk.

HMS *Bath*: A Newport-class destroyer built in the USA, this ship was transferred to the Royal Navy in 1940. She saw active service in the Second World War and was later transferred to the Royal Norwegian Navy. She was named for the town in New York State and for Bath, Somerset.

Bath Bricks: These were neither invented nor manufactured in the city. They were made from fine river clay, and produced by several companies in the Bridgwater area of Somerset. Bath Bricks were used for sharpening and, when powdered, for scouring – the forerunners of Vim and Ajax. They were patented in the 1820s, and given their name because their colour after firing resembles that of Bath stone.

ANAGRAMMATIC BATH

Rearranging the letters of the names of some locations in Bath can produce curious results. Here are a few examples:

Bath Abbey = Bathe baby
Richard 'Beau' Nash = Hair care husband
John Wood, architect = Joined watch cohort
Royal Victoria Park = Or a prickly aviator
Roman Baths Museum = Mum bust a horseman
Great Pulteney St = Astutely peg rent
The Assembly Rooms = Sombrely smash toe

Pulteney Bridge = Prudently beige
Bath Spa Station = A botanist's path
Holburne Museum = Our humble menus
Parade Gardens = Draper's agenda
Pierrepont Street = I represent potter
The King's Circus = Skiing crutches
Kingsmead Square = Made Quakers sing
John Wood the Younger = Good journey when hot

and my own favourite:

Royal Crescent = Larceny sector

2

PEOPLE

THEY CAME FROM BATH

Those who are native to, or live in, Bath are known as 'Bathonians'. Here are a few well-known people who were actually born here:

Bill Bailey, actor and comedian
Mary Berry, cookery expert
Jennifer Biddall, actor (*Hollyoaks*)
Jeremy Guscott, Bath and England rugby union player
Barbara Leigh-Hunt, stage and TV actor
Jonathan Lynn, actor and writer (*Yes, Minister*)
Kris Marshall, actor (*Death in Paradise*)
Harry Patch, the 'Last Fighting Tommy'
Arnold Ridley, playwright and actor (*Dad's Army*)
John Arthur Roebuck Rudge, pioneer of cinematography
Ann Widdecombe, politician
Jacqueline Wilson, author

(Incidentally, 'Bathonian' is also a geological term given to a stage of the Middle Jurassic period – about 170 million years ago.)

THEY CAME TO BATH – BUT NEVER LEFT!

Some of the notable people who died in the city:

Revd George Austen (1731–1805): Father of the novelist Jane. He was rector of Steventon in Hampshire but after his retirement the family moved to Bath in 1801. He died in 1805 and is buried in the crypt of St Swithin's, Walcot.

Senator William Bingham (1752–1804): Born in Pennsylvania, USA, he served on the US Senate from 1795 to 1801 and helped broker the Louisiana Purchase. He came to England after the death of his wife and died while on a visit to Bath. He is buried in the abbey where there is a monument to his memory.

Frances 'Fanny' Burney (1752–1840): Novelist, diarist and playwright. Her first novel, *Evelina*, was published in 1778. After her marriage (1793) she became Madame d'Arblay. She is buried in Walcot cemetery.

Sarah Fielding (1710–68): The sister of Henry Fielding, author of *Tom Jones*. Herself an author, she wrote *The Adventures of David Simple* and other works. She has a plaque in the abbey.

Admiral Sir William Hargood (1762–1839): A veteran of the Battle of Trafalgar (1805), where he commanded HMS *Belleisle*. He was knighted by George III in 1815 and lived in the Royal Crescent from 1834 until his death.

Richard 'Beau' Nash (1674–1761): Master of Ceremonies in Bath for more than fifty years. The arbiter of taste and elegance in the city, he drew up codes of dress and behaviour which were adopted throughout the country. Nicknamed 'the King of Bath', he controlled the social side of things and earned the respect of visitors from all levels of society. At his death he was honoured with a splendid civic funeral, and has a memorial tablet in Bath Abbey.

James Quin (1693–1766): A famous Georgian actor, celebrated for his portrayal of Shakespeare's Falstaff. He is buried in Bath Abbey, where there is a plaque with an inscription written by his friend and fellow actor David Garrick.

Admiral Arthur Phillip (1738–1814): Commander of the First Fleet to Australia, he was the first Governor of New South Wales and founder of the settlement which became Sydney. He retired to Bath, where he died, and is reputedly buried in the churchyard of St Nicholas, Bathampton, although some doubt has now been cast over whether the body is actually there. However, the church does contain an Australia Chapel.

Sir Isaac Pitman (1813–97): The inventor of Pitman's Shorthand. He lived at No. 17 Royal Crescent. Even at the age of 84 he could be found at his desk every morning at 6.30. He is also buried in Bath Abbey.

… AND SOME BATHONIANS WHO (PROBABLY) NEVER WERE!

Prince Bladud: According to legend, he discovered the curative powers of Bath's springs. Having contracted leprosy, he became a swineherd, and transmitted the disease to the pigs. One day, on reaching the hot springs in the Avon valley, his pigs wallowed in the steamy waters and their skins rapidly improved. He bathed in the springs himself and was cured of the terrible disease from which he had been suffering. Returning to court, he eventually succeeded his father as King, and went on to found the city of Bath in gratitude for his good fortune. He is said to have been the father of King Lear. His story does not end well, however, as he was later killed while attempting to fly with a pair of homemade wings. In 2008 there was a public art event in the city in which over 100 'Bladud's Pigs', sculpted in resin and painted by local artists, were displayed around the city before being auctioned. Over £200,000 was raised for Bath's 'Two Tunnels' project.

Charlotte Brunswick: Chocolatier. The shop in Church Street that bears her name sells high-quality handcrafted chocolates, and was opened in 2013. Charlotte herself is an imaginary eighteenth-century character, invented by the owners as an 'identity' around which to base their products. She is portrayed as having been born in Bath into a wealthy family, from whom she inherited an enquiring mind and love of exploration. The name 'Brunswick' was chosen as it is an old Bath name, still to be found in the city today.

Sally Lunn: Pastry cook and the supposed inventor of the famous bun that bears her name. Tradition says that she was a Huguenot refugee who came to Bath in the seventeenth century, bringing with her the recipe for 'Sally Lunns' and setting up her business in what is now North Parade Passage. Research has so far, however, failed to find any positive proof that she ever existed. Happily, the buns definitely do, but if you want the secret recipe, you'll have to buy the business!

Sulis: The name of the goddess the ancient Celts believed was the guardian of the sacred springs, hence the Roman name for Bath: 'Aquae Sulis'. The Romans conflated her with one of their own goddesses, Minerva, and dedicated the temple jointly to the two deities. The mysterious 'Gorgon's Head' motif on the temple pediment is thought to be partly an indirect reference to Sulis.

IT TAKES ALL SORTS

Some of the notable and eccentric characters who have enriched Bath's history:

William Beckford (1760–1844): The son of a wealthy Lord Mayor of London who owned sugar plantations in the Caribbean. On his father's death he became probably the richest man in England. He built Fonthill Abbey, an enormous Gothic folly in Wiltshire. During his residence there he became involved in a scandal concerning a relationship with a young male cousin, and Beckford and his wife went into self-imposed exile on the Continent for several years. In 1824 he moved to Bath, buying two houses in Lansdown Crescent, where he became known as a respectable, though rarely seen, eccentric, sometimes referred to as 'the Fool of Fonthill'. There he remained until his death, spending his time in writing and collecting works of art. He built Beckford's Tower on Lansdown Hill, which he used as a retreat, and he is buried in a massive granite sarcophagus nearby.

Eli Collins (?–2014): known locally as 'Mad Eli', Collins was a former professional wrestler and promoter who, for more than twenty years, devoted himself to fundraising for charity. The basement area of his flat in Johnstone Street was filled with toys, and passers-by would throw in their loose change, which would be passed on to various local charities. He would also arrange impromptu events such as wrestling matches and tabletop sales. He is estimated to have raised over £3.5 million for good causes.

Philip Thicknesse (1719–92): Born in Staffordshire, Thicknesse became a soldier of fortune, and secured the governorship of the Landguard Fort at Harwich. Twice married, he moved to Bath and occupied a house in the Royal Crescent, becoming well known for his eccentricity and his ill-tempered nature. He had previously befriended the young Thomas Gainsborough and persuaded him to further his artistic career by moving to Bath (although the two men later quarrelled). Thicknesse was the author of *The New Prose Bath Guide*, a description of the city and its ways. To his disappointment, the book was not a great success.

Selina, Countess of Huntingdon (1707–91): Born Lady Selina Shirley, she became a countess on her marriage in 1728 to Theophilus Hastings, 9th Earl of Huntingdon. In London she joined the first Methodist society and after her husband's death became involved with the work of the Wesley brothers and George Whitefield in the Methodist movement. After disagreements on points of doctrine, she formed her own 'Connexion', establishing no less than sixty-four chapels, including the one in Bath, where she was a vigorous opponent of Beau Nash and the lifestyle he represented.

'Guinea Pig Jack' (1848–1907): Born Dominico Conio in Italy, he came to Bath in 1848 at the age of 16. He began by selling newspapers around the city, but discovered that he could make more money by training small pets such as guinea pigs to perform a variety of tricks, and would set up his show on street corners for the entertainment of passers-by. He died in 1907.

Margaret Forbes Fraser: The daughter of an eminent Bath surgeon after whom a ward at the Royal United Hospital is named. During the 1940s she became well known for riding to work on a horse. In later life she would often be seen about the city in her invariable garb of purple pop socks and desert boots.

Amabel Wellesley-Colley (1907–87): The lady who, in 1971, famously caused a furore by painting the white front door of her house, No. 22 Royal Crescent, primrose yellow. When ordered by the City Council to return it to its original colour, the lady (a descendant of the Duke of Wellington, no less) refused, and fought her case through to the High Court in London. She eventually won it when the then Secretary of State for the Environment ruled in 1977 that the door could remain yellow – as it has to this day.

TEN THINGS YOU MIGHT NOT KNOW ABOUT RICHARD 'BEAU' NASH

1. He was a Welshman, born on 18 October 1674 in Swansea, where his father (also Richard) was a partner in a glassmaking company.

2. He attended Jesus College, Oxford, where he studied law, but left without obtaining a degree. This was not uncommon in the eighteenth century.

3. In 1705 he came to Bath, where his natural aptitude for gambling, together with his notable style and manner, made him a social success.

4. He became the understudy to the Master of the Ceremonies, a Captain Webster. Following Webster's death in a duel, Nash succeeded to the post, which he held for more than fifty years.

5. Nash appears (briefly) in Book XI, Chapter IV of Henry Fielding's famous novel *Tom Jones* and is also mentioned in some of the 'Bath' novels of Georgette Heyer.

6. During his tenure as Master of Ceremonies, he kept more than one mistress (though not all at once!). When accused of being a 'whoremonger', he replied, 'A man can no more be termed a whoremonger for having one whore in his house, than a cheesemonger for having one cheese.'

7. A cinema in Westgate Street was for many years called the 'Beau Nash'. It is now the Komedia Comedy Club and is a Grade II listed building. There is also an antique and silverware shop in Brock Street called 'Beau Nash'.

8. Nash also held the post of Master of Ceremonies at Tunbridge Wells, Kent, and would travel between the two locations by coach. A pub in the town is named after him.

9. Some of the incidents of Nash's life, including his army career, cannot be verified from records and may have been invented by the man himself or by his chroniclers.

10. It is not known for certain where Beau Nash is buried, as the Corporation of Bath only gave money for his funeral and not for his burial. His plaque in the abbey is merely a memorial.

ROYAL VISITORS TO BATH

Over the centuries Bath has hosted many royal visitors. Here are some of them.

Edgar (reigned 959–75): Known as 'the Peaceful', and often regarded as the first King of a united England, his coronation took place in the first Bath Abbey in AD 973, near the end of his reign. The service, devised by Dunstan, Archbishop of Canterbury, formed the basis of that which is still used for British coronations today.

Edward the Confessor (reigned 1042–66): He visited Bath in 1061 with his wife, Edith of Wessex.

Henry I (reigned 1100–35): He held his Easter Council at Bath in 1106.

Matilda of Boulogne (*c.* 1105–52): Queen to King Stephen (reigned 1135–54). She came to Bath in 1140 to represent her husband in the peace conference which had been arranged to take place there. The talks broke up without a settlement, leading to civil war.

John (reigned 1189–1216): John visited Bath on four occasions between 1209 and 1216, staying at the Royal Lodgings or the Bishop's Chambers.

Henry III (reigned 1216–72): He paid a state visit to Bath in 1235.

Edward I (reigned 1272–1307): He visited the city in 1276 during an inspection of his property.

Richard II (reigned 1377–99): Richard visited Bath as a boy, but was apparently unimpressed.

Henry VI (reigned 1422–61): Henry's personal confessor, John Blacman, relates how the naïve and pious King visited the warm spa at Bath, where he was shocked by the sight of naked men. Blacman tells us, 'He was displeased, and went away quickly, abhorring such nudity as a great offence'. The date of this visit is not recorded. His wife, Margaret of Anjou, visited in 1471 in an (unsuccessful) attempt to raise Bath to her cause of restoring her husband to the throne.

Edward IV (reigned 1461–83): He marched on Bath in 1471 in an attempt to forestall Margaret and stayed one night in the city.

Henry VII (reigned 1485–1509): Henry came to Bath on three occasions. In 1496 he stopped on his way to Bristol, where he gave his blessing to the explorer John Cabot. His formal visit the following year was an occasion of great splendour, commemorated in the Bath Pageant of 1909.

Elizabeth I (reigned 1558–1603): 'Good Queen Bess' visited the city in 1574 and a good deal of money was spent on improvements before her visit. The corporation even sent to Tetbury and Cirencester (Gloucestershire) for men to pave some of the streets in readiness for her arrival. The abbey was decorated with greenery in an attempt to disguise its (then) sorry appearance. Sixteen years later, the Queen granted the city a new charter.

Anne of Denmark (1574–1619): The Queen to James I came to the city twice, in 1613 and 1615. This unfortunate lady suffered from dropsy and maintained that the Bath waters helped alleviate her condition.

Charles I (reigned 1625–49): Charles visited Bath in 1628 and his Queen, Henrietta Maria, stayed for a few days in 1644 due to the worsening military situation of the English Civil War.

Charles II (reigned 1660–85): He and his Queen, Catherine of Braganza, first came to Bath in 1677, hoping that a course of the waters would help her to produce an heir to the throne. This proved to be unsuccessful, even though they did visit the city on future occasions.

James II (reigned 1685–88): He came to Bath, together with his Queen, Mary of Modena, in 1687, also in the hope that she would produce a male child. Unlike their predecessors, they were successful and Mary was delivered of a son the following year. He was James Edward Stuart (the 'Old Pretender'). His father was deposed in the same year.

Anne (reigned 1702–14): Anne visited Bath on four occasions, twice when she was still a princess, and twice (1702 and 1703) after she became Queen. She suffered badly from gout, and came to take the waters in the hope of obtaining relief. She was accompanied on the two latter occasions by her husband, Prince George of Denmark.

William IV, Prince of Orange (the Dutch Royal House): He visited the city twice in 1734, once prior to his marriage to the Princess Anne, daughter of George II, and again with his new wife soon after their marriage. His health was poor and he suffered from curvature of the spine. The Orange Grove behind the abbey, with its obelisk (commissioned by Beau Nash), is named after him.

Frederick Louis, Prince of Wales: The eldest son of George II, paid Bath a visit in 1738, when he was accompanied by his wife, Augusta. He visited again in 1750. Nicknamed 'Poor Fred', he was disliked by his parents and never succeeded to the throne, dying in 1751 from an abscess on the lung. An obelisk in Queen Square, also commissioned by Nash and with an inscription by Alexander Pope, commemorates the 1738 visit.

Napoleon III (Louis-Napoléon Bonaparte, 1808–73): The nephew of Napoleon Bonaparte, and Emperor of France from 1852 to 1870, visited Bath on several occasions, staying at the Sydney Hotel and later in Great Pulteney Street.

Victoria (reigned 1837–1901): Victoria first visited the city in 1830, at the age of 11. She was accompanied by her mother, the Duchess of Kent, and they stayed at what is now the Royal York Hotel on the corner of George Street and Broad Street. A long-held local tradition tells how she took offence at a personal remark she overheard from someone in the crowd and refused ever to visit the city again, ordering the carriage blinds drawn if the train ever passed through! The truth, however, is that she later declared that she had enjoyed her visit, particularly her ride in a sedan chair. It is also recorded that, on a later occasion when the train was passing through Bath, it slowed down so that she could wave to the crowds.

Haile Selassie (1892–1975): The Emperor of Ethiopia, spent a period of exile in Bath between 1936 and 1940, following the occupation of his country by the Italians. He received the Freedom of the City when he returned for a state visit in 1954.

Elizabeth II (reigned 1952–): Her Majesty first visited Bath with Prince Philip, Duke of Edinburgh, in 1956. She also attended a lunch at Bath's Guildhall in 1977 as part of her Silver Jubilee celebrations. Her parents and grandparents both visited the city: George V and Queen Mary in 1917 and George VI and Queen Elizabeth in 1942, shortly after the Bath Blitz.

ADELARD OF BATH

Asked to name some famous personages who have been associated with the history of Bath, very few people would come up with the name of Adelard. Even some who have heard of him might confuse him with Peter Abelard, the twelfth-century monk who became the ill-fated lover of Heloise.

Adelard of Bath was born in the city in about 1080. His father worked in the household of Giso, Bishop of Wells; of his mother nothing is known. In 1088 John of Tours became Bishop of Bath and Wells and took the young Adelard under his wing. A bright child, Adelard studied in Bath at the school founded by the bishop and then at the University of Tours. He travelled extensively throughout the Middle East, studying philosophy, mathematics, astronomy, astrology and languages, including Arabic and its number system. He returned to Bath in 1116, where his skills and knowledge made him an important figure. He was introduced at court and may have become a tutor to the young Henry II.

Adelard has been called England's first true scientist. He wrote a book in which he attempted to answer many questions about the natural world, and his book was one of the first to be printed some 300 years later. He is believed to have died some time around 1160, but the location of his burial is unknown.

WHAT THEY SAID ABOUT BATH

Some comments about the city by people who knew it well:

'There is always the Town at command and the Countryside for prospect, exercise and delight.' (Fanny Burney)

'The town most of stone and clean, though the streets generally narrow.' (Samuel Pepys)

'A place that helps the indolent and gay to commit the worst of all murder – to kill time!' (Daniel Defoe)

'I know of no better place than Bath for an old cock to roost in.' (James Quin)

'We are a verie little poore Citie, our Clothmen much decay'd.' (Robert Fry, Mayor of Bath 1622)

'The last place of our baths, is a citie in Summersetshire, which taketh his name of the hot waters there to be seen and used.' (Raphael Holinshed, 1577)

'They may say what they will, but it does one ten times more good to leave Bath than to go to it.' (Horace Walpole)

'In a word, 'tis a Vale of Pleasure, yet a Sink of Iniquity.' (Ned Ward)

'You know, this is like Jamaica to any other part of England.' (Horatio Nelson)

'Of the many beautiful cities in this fair country, Bath is unquestionably the most beautiful.' (Sir Isaac Pitman)

'Bath spread herself before us, like a beautiful dowager giving a reception.' (J.B. Priestley)

'Bath is where the young cannot live, and the old cannot die.' (G.K. Chesterton)

'Bath looks to me like a cemetery, which the dead have succeeded in rising and taking.' (Charles Dickens)

'It's a nice town, but back home we bury our dead.' (Twentieth-century American visitor to Bath)

'Can the Gospel have place where Satan's Throne is?' (John Wesley)

'Bath is one of the most beautiful cities in Europe.' (Joseph Haydn)

3

GETTING AROUND

TRANSPORT

The most popular mode of transport around the city in Georgian times, for those who preferred not to walk, was the sedan chair. Basically an enclosed box with windows and a seat, it could accommodate one person at a time, and was carried on horizontal poles by two men. Its name does not come, as some have suggested, from the town of Sedan in France, but from the Latin *sedere*, meaning 'to sit'. They were also sometimes known as 'glass chairs'. In Bath, sedan chairs had the right of way over pedestrians, who were expected to flatten themselves against a wall when a chair came by. Until Beau Nash's time, fares were not fixed, nor the chairmen regulated, and many of them had gained a bad reputation for coarse or threatening behaviour. Nash insisted that they should be licensed, with a recognised tariff of fares. Queen's Parade Place includes the only examples in Britain of sedan chair houses, where chairmen could wait or rest between fares. Some of the larger houses in Bath were built with especially wide staircases so that the chairmen could carry their passenger directly to his or her room.

There was a special type of sedan chair which was adapted for use by patients at the Mineral Water Hospital. It had shorter poles and looked a bit like an upright coffin with a bulge at the front to allow space for the feet of patients suffering from gout.

The sedan chair was eventually superseded by the Bath Chair, which was probably invented by John Dawson of Bath, although another Bathonian, James Heath, has also been claimed as its inventor. The Bath chair was a (normally) three-wheeled contrivance for one person. It had a folding hood, and could either be steered by the passenger with a second person pushing, or both pulled and steered by one person. It became very popular in the early nineteenth century, and its use continued into the twentieth. In his book, *In Search of England* (1927), H.V. Morton describes how, on wet days, the chairmen would sit inside their chairs, waiting for customers. The last Bath chairman retired in 1948.

There were many livery stables in the city from which horses could be hired for 'riding out' (the ladies, of course, riding side saddle). Riding lessons were available for those who had not mastered the skill. Carriages of all types were also available for hire, although many residents (and visitors) would possess their own. Young men (the equivalent of today's 'boy racers') would sometimes hold unofficial 'gig races' along wide thoroughfares such as Great Pulteney Street, although this was frowned upon. Even in Georgian and Regency Bath traffic was already becoming a problem. Jane Austen (in *Northanger Abbey*) complains that Cheap Street is 'a street of so impertinent a nature ... that a day never passes in which parties of ladies ... are not detained upon one side or other by carriages, horsemen or carts.' She would be astonished (and probably even more annoyed) by the traffic in Bath today.

Today, Bath has an efficient bus service, and taxis have, of course, replaced the sedan and Bath Chairs. Many visitors use the red open-top buses, which offer sightseeing tours of the city and its immediate environs. There are also companies that offer horse-drawn carriage tours, and even tours by 'tuk tuk', which can reach places that are inaccessible to coaches.

Another way of seeing the city, this time from the air, is by hot-air balloon. There are several companies offering flights, some throughout the year, which take off from Royal Victoria Park and afford spectacular views of Bath.

Launched in 2014, a more energetic way of seeing the city is by using Nextbikes, a series of cycle stations in the city from which bicycles can be hired and returned. There are currently nine stations and 100 bikes for hire, available 24 hours a day. Registration and payment are by credit card. One wonders what Miss Austen would have made of that!

Before the coming of the railways and improvements to roads, the river Avon was an important artery of communication, particularly between Bath and Bristol. Today, pleasure craft will take the visitor on trips by water through the city and its surroundings.

One of the best ways to see Bath is, of course, on foot; indeed, there are many areas that can only be seen properly in this way. Walking tours of the city are offered by a number of agencies, with various 'themed' walks (e.g. Jane Austen, ghosts, quirky and offbeat etc.) available. The Mayor of Bath's Honorary Corps of Guides, which has been operating in the city for about eighty years, offers free, two-hour guided walks around the city twice daily (except on Christmas Day).

GATES OF BATH, PAST AND PRESENT

Like many cities, Bath was surrounded in medieval times by a wall, in which were positioned four principal gateways, located in the north, east, south and west sections of the wall.

The North Gate was the one used by travellers from London and the north of the country. It was 10ft (3m) wide and 15ft (4.5m) in height and housed a dungeon, armoury and soldiers' quarters. Long since demolished, it stood at the present-day junction of Upper Borough Walls and High Street.

The West Gate would be entered by travellers from Bristol and other points west. It was rebuilt in 1572 in readiness for the visit of Elizabeth I, and subsequently enlarged. It also had rooms that provided lodgings for some eighteenth-century royal visitors. This gate, too, no longer exists, but is commemorated in the name of Westgate Street.

The South Gate was, by all accounts, the most imposing of the city's gates, being adorned with statues, which included one of Edward III. The name has been retained as the title of the modern shopping centre near the railway station.

The smaller and less elaborate East Gate is the only one still existing, and can be seen today behind the former Empire Hotel and below present-day ground level. This gate would once have led to the former Boatstall Quay and a ferry crossing of the Avon. Unlike the other city gates it would have remained open at night, except in time of war.

The green and gold wrought-iron gates at either end of Royal Avenue are modern replicas, replacing the Victorian originals that were taken away in 1942 to support the war effort. The gate pillars at the western end are surmounted by a pair of sphinxes, while those at the eastern (Queen's Gate) end have lions, each resting a paw on an orb.

ON THE RAILS

The coming of the railway to Bath in the nineteenth century made a considerable difference to the city's fortunes. Bath Spa Station opened in August 1840 as part of the Great Western Railway linking London and Bristol and is a Grade II* listed building. The chief engineer for the GWR project was Isambard Kingdom Brunel and the station (which he designed) is in a Tudor-Gothic style. The railway originally operated on the broad-gauge (7ft) system, only converting to standard gauge in 1892. The fastest journey time between London and Bristol in 1841 was 4 hours 10 minutes, and the third-class passengers travelled in open carriages (it's recorded that one man died of exposure!).

Opposite the front of the station were two almost-matching hotels on the corners of Manvers Street: the Argyle and the Royal (originally the 'George'). The Argyle has since been converted for retail use, but the Royal is still a hotel and was once linked to the station by a high-level footbridge. Both hotels were intended to complete the Manvers Street approach to the station, which was laid out in accordance with the Great Western Railway Act of 1835.

UNDERGROUND BATH

The former stone mines in the hills overlooking the city consist of many underground passages from which Bath stone has been extracted for centuries. The first evidence of its use dates from Roman times and it continued to be used throughout the Middle Ages. In the eighteenth century, Ralph Allen acquired mines on Combe and Bathampton Downs and promoted extensive use of the stone. Gradually the mines were worked out, although mining work still continues in the Corsham (Wiltshire) area, but on a much smaller scale than previously.

Since mining operations ceased, some of the shafts and tunnels have been used for a variety of purposes. They were employed as air-raid shelters and as places for stockpiling munitions and storing art objects during the Second World War and, more recently, for the growing of mushrooms. Some have become homes for large populations of bats, including both the Greater and Lesser Horseshoe bat.

The area between Terrace Walk and Parade Gardens is known as 'Bog Island' (from the rather impolite name for a toilet). The underground public conveniences located here, built in the 1930s, later became one of Bath's most popular nightclubs. Nowadays the facility has become unsafe and is empty and abandoned.

Bath's 'Two Tunnels' circuit, which is part of the National Cycle Network, was opened in April 2013. It is a 13-mile (21km) cycling and walking route, which includes two former railway tunnels, the Combe Down Tunnel and the Devonshire Tunnel at Bloomfield. The former, at just over a mile long, is the longest tunnel for cyclists and walkers in the UK, and was once part of the Somerset and Dorset Railway line. It has LED lighting and a special surface for cyclists.

In 1994 the restored eighteenth-century cellars of Bath Abbey were opened as a Heritage Museum, featuring many exhibits and artefacts exploring the abbey's history and development. Because the Roman street level of Bath was about 16ft (5m) below present-day ground level, the museum, with the baths and all the exhibits, lies underground, extending beneath Abbey Churchyard and Kingston Parade. Excavation was begun in the late nineteenth century and continued, on and off, until well into the twentieth. At the time of writing the museum is closed for redevelopment.

Once the thermal waters had passed through the Baths complex, they ran away through the Great Drain to the river, about 450 yards (400m) away. This was sufficiently high to allow a man to walk through without stooping, so that Roman engineers could regularly clear the drain of sediment. The drain is still fulfilling its original purpose and can be seen in the Roman Baths Museum.

WATERWAYS OF BATH

The river Avon that flows through Bath is sometimes known as the Lower or Bristol Avon, to distinguish it from the Warwickshire or 'Shakespeare's' Avon or any of the three other English rivers of the same name. The Bristol Avon rises just north of the village of Acton Turville in Gloucestershire, flows through the cities of Bath and Bristol and finally enters the Severn Estuary at Avonmouth. It is 75 miles (121km) in length and the stretch from Bath to the sea is known as the Avon Navigation. This stretch was an important artery for trade in the eighteenth century, being used to transport luxury goods coming in through the port of Bristol upriver to fashionable Georgian Bath.

The Kennet and Avon Canal was engineered by John Rennie and opened in 1810. This provided a means to transport goods from Bath or Bristol all the way to London. The canal was designed to link the Bristol Avon at Bath with the river Kennet at Newbury, and thence to Reading on the Thames. Its length is 87 miles (140km) with 105 locks, and it took sixteen years to complete. With the coming of the Great Western Railway its revenue declined, and the GWR eventually took it over. The canal became disused and overgrown, but in the 1960s the K&A Canal Trust was formed and over the years the canal has been restored and is now fully open. Queen Elizabeth performed the reopening ceremony in 1990. The towpath is popular with walkers and cyclists, and the George Inn at Bathampton is a very good place for what the author Jerome K. Jerome once described as 'a rest, and other things'.

STREETS NAMED AFTER NOTABLE PEOPLE

Alfred Street: Alfred the Great, King of Wessex (871–99), defeated the Danish invaders at the battles of Ashdown and Edington.

Beau Street: Richard 'Beau' Nash (1674–1761), famous arbiter of taste and fashion, and Master of Ceremonies in Bath for more than fifty years.

Beckford Road: William Beckford (1760–1844), author and eccentric, was known as 'England's Wealthiest Son'. He came to Bath in 1822 and lived in Lansdown Crescent.

Brock Street: Thomas Brock was the brother-in-law of John Wood the Younger and sometime Town Clerk of Chester.

Charlotte Street: Charlotte of Mecklenburg-Strelitz (1744–1818) was Queen to George III. Married in 1761, they met for the first time on their wedding day.

Chatham Row: Originally called Pitt Street, it was named for William Pitt the Elder, sometime MP for Bath. The name was changed when he was created Earl of Chatham in 1766.

Harington Place: Sir John Harington (1560–1612) was a godson of Elizabeth I and designer of Britain's first flushing toilet. He lived at Kelston, near Bath, and kept a townhouse in the city.

Ivo Peters Road: Ivo Peters BEM (1915–89), a long-time resident of Bath, became famous for his photographs and films of steam railways, particularly the Somerset and Dorset.

Monmouth Street: James Scott, 1st Duke of Monmouth (1649–85), was an illegitimate son of King Charles II. He led the ill-fated Monmouth Rebellion in 1685, by which he hoped to depose Charles's brother, King James II.

Nelson Place: Admiral Horatio Nelson (1758–1805) was the great naval commander and national hero. He was killed at the Battle of Trafalgar.

Orange Grove: Prince William of Orange, of the Dutch royal family, came to Bath in 1734 to take the waters. The obelisk in the centre marks this visit.

Queen Square: Caroline of Ansbach (1683–1737) was Queen to George II. The obelisk in the centre marks the visit of their son Frederick, Prince of Wales, in 1738.

Ralph Allen Drive: Ralph Allen (1693–1764) was the builder of Prior Park. He owned stone mines above Bath, which supplied much of the Bath stone used in the city.

Sydney Place: Thomas Townshend, 1st Viscount Sydney (1733–1800), was the British Home Secretary from 1782–89. Sydney, Australia and Sydney, Nova Scotia are named in his honour.

Wood Street and John Street: John Wood the Elder (1704–54), was the famous architect who designed some of Bath's most notable architecture (Queen Square, The Circus, etc.).

STREETS WITH CURIOUS NAMES …

Boatstall Lane: This steep alleyway led down via the East Gate to the river Avon. Before the completion of Pulteney Bridge in 1774, the only means of crossing the river to reach Spring Gardens was by ferryboat. It can be seen today behind the Guildhall.

Brassknocker Hill: On the edge of the city, this leads up to Claverton Down. It gained its name in coaching days, when extra horses were needed to help ascend the steep gradient. At the bottom of the hill were the stables where there was a large brass doorknocker, which could be used to summon the stable lads.

Broad Street: Perplexingly, this one-way street is quite narrow. It gets its name from the fact that it was once an area largely occupied by Bath's weavers, who produced high-quality broadcloth.

Comfortable Place: This is located on the Upper Bristol Road (A4), opposite Royal Victoria Park.

Holloway: This is probably a corruption of 'Holy Way' and lies along the route once taken by pilgrims and other travellers to Glastonbury.

Hot Bath Street: This was named for its proximity to the Hot Bath, site of one of the city's three thermal springs.

Nowhere Place: Located near Southgate Buildings, according to local tradition, this area gained its nickname because servant girls would meet their male friends here. When asked by their employer where they had been, they would reply, 'Oh, nowhere'.

Old Lilliput Alley: The former name of what is now, more prosaically, called North Parade Passage.

Oolite Grove, Odd Down: This is named after the oolite ('egg stone'), the sedimentary limestone rock of which local Bath stone is composed.

Perfect View: Located off Camden Road, looking across towards Bathampton, it featured in Rory Bremner's ITV series *Great British Views* (2013).

Slippery Lane. Originally known as Alford Lane, this was a steep medieval thoroughfare which led down to a ford, and later a ferry, which once crossed the river. Now called Northgate Lane, it can be seen near the Podium Shopping Centre. The ferry was eventually superseded by Pulteney Bridge.

Titan Barrow, Bathford: Named after the house built by John Wood the Elder for Southwell Pigott, Esquire, in 1748.

Vineyards: This area, on the west side of The Paragon, was formerly a vineyard until building leases were granted in 1759.

... AND STREETS THAT NEVER WERE!

Any visitor to Bath who tries to find Great Annandale Street or Frances Square is doomed to disappointment, as, although planned, they were never built! They were part of the scheme for the development of land east of the Avon at a time when Bath was expanding rapidly. Once the Pulteney Bridge had been completed in 1774, this land was ripe for the building of a new estate, to be known as Bathwick New Town. The landowner, Sir William Pulteney, engaged the services of Thomas Baldwin, the City Architect, to design the estate, which would contain a large square, a new crescent and many fine streets, with Great

Pulteney Street as the 'spine' road. However, in the 1790s, with England at war with France, the threat of a French invasion brought about a crisis of confidence and the collapse of several banks, resulting in the abandonment of the rest of the project. The 'stumps' of some of the side streets still remain (see Sunderland Street), with Bath Rugby Club occupying the area originally intended for the crescent, and Henrietta Park on what was to have been Frances Square.

BRIDGING THE GAPS

Some of the most important bridges spanning waterways and railways in Bath are as follows:

Pulteney Bridge is the most famous in the city and spans the Avon near the Guildhall Market. Built in 1774 to the design of Robert Adam, the Italianate bridge connected the old city with the new development at Bathwick. It is the only bridge of its kind in Britain, having shops down its full length on both sides. Adam is said to have taken his inspiration from bridges such as Florence's Ponte Vecchio. The little domed buildings at each end were once tollhouses. The weir just below the bridge was completed in 1972 as part of the city's flood control measures.

North Parade Bridge, a little farther along the river, dates from 1836 and was originally a cast-iron structure. Before it was built, North Parade was (like South Parade today) a cul-de-sac. There are two lodges on the bridge, where tolls were once collected.

Cleveland Bridge is downriver of the other two, and, like them, was once a toll bridge. The date on the bridge (in Roman numerals) is 1827, and the bridge is named after the Duke of Cleveland, who was then the Lord of the Manor. It is believed that the spot where the Romans originally had a ferry crossing is nearby.

The Widcombe footbridge is also known as the 'Halfpenny Bridge', after the original toll charged for pedestrians. It crosses the river behind Bath Spa Railway Station, and was built in 1862. In 1877 it was the scene of a tragedy when the bridge collapsed while crowded with people trying to get to the Bath and West Show. At least ten people died and more than fifty were injured.

Churchill Bridge is a relatively new structure, built in 1964–66. It replaced the Old Bridge, which dated from 1304 and had a chapel and a tower with portcullis on it, giving access to the old South Gate of the city. The bridge was originally to be called Southgate Bridge, but was instead named after Sir Winston Churchill, whose death coincided with its construction.

The 'Skew' bridge, behind Bath Spa Station, was built by Isambard Kingdom Brunel in 1840 to carry his Great Western Railway across the river. Originally of timber, it was rebuilt in the 1870s with wrought-iron girders.

New Bridge is east of Bath on the road to Bristol. Actually the oldest surviving bridge in Bath, it was originally built with three arches in 1736, the river Avon having been made navigable between Bristol and Bath in 1727. It was rebuilt with a single arch in the late eighteenth century and has been strengthened in modern times.

Victoria Bridge spans the Avon alongside the Bristol–Bath road. A Grade II listed structure, it was built in 1836 to a design by James Dredge, a local brewer. It is known as a 'taper' suspension bridge and uses chains rather than cables. It was the first bridge of its type in the world. Declared unsafe in 2010, it was reopened in 2015 after a £3.4 million refurbishment.

In the grounds of Prior Park is a Palladian-style bridge, spanning a small lake. This was built by Ralph Allen's Clerk of Works, Richard Jones, and is a close copy of a bridge at Wilton House, Wiltshire.

SLIGHTLY FARTHER AFIELD

As Bath grew, it gradually absorbed a number of nearby villages, which are now suburbs of the city.

Widcombe: The name means 'wide combe' (or valley) and it lies across the Avon to the south-east, where the Kennet and Avon Canal joins the river Avon. The Domesday Survey mentions a small settlement here, although nothing of it can be seen today. Worth seeing is Widcombe Manor House, dating from 1656 and rebuilt in 1727 by the Bennet family, whose crest can be seen at the entrance gates. Once the home of the novelist Horace Annesley Vachell, it was later owned by the entrepreneur Jeremy Fry, who frequently entertained Princess Margaret and her husband, Anthony Armstrong-Jones. Also nearby is the late fifteenth-century church of St Thomas à Becket, which took the place of a previous Norman church. There may even have been a Saxon chapel on the site. Widcombe Crescent (1808) is a Georgian terrace of fourteen houses by Bath architect Thomas Baldwin.

Batheaston: As its name suggests, Batheaston stands to the east of the city and is also mentioned in Domesday Book, where it is called 'Estone'. It is overlooked by the Iron Age hill fort of Solsbury Hill, which was occupied between the third and first centuries BC. The church of St John the Baptist dates from the twelfth century (remodelled in the fifteenth). Eagle House (built in the early eighteenth century) was for a time the home of John Wood the Younger, and he died there in 1782.

Bathampton: Bathampton is linked to Batheaston by a toll bridge which crosses the Avon. Above the village is Sham Castle, a folly built for Ralph Allen in 1762. The church of St Nicholas was built in the thirteenth and fifteenth centuries and contains an 'Australia Chapel' with memorials to Arthur Phillip, first Governor of New South Wales, who is believed to be buried here. The churchyard contains the grave of Vicomte du Barré, killed in a duel in 1778. Between 1900 and 1983 Plasticine was manufactured in Bathampton; its inventor, William Harbutt, lived in the village.

Bathford: Bathford takes its name from the ford that crossed the By Brook and was once part of the Roman Fosse Way. The ford was replaced in the fourteenth century by the bridge which still stands. On the hill above is Brown's Folly, a tower erected in 1840 by Wade Brown, a local quarry owner.

Claverton and Claverton Down: Claverton (from Old English, meaning 'clover') is a small village east of Bath and was designated a Conservation Area in 1981. The church of St Mary the Virgin has a Norman tower; the rest is mostly thirteenth century but extensive restoration was carried out in the mid-1850s. Ralph Allen is buried in a pyramid-topped mausoleum in the churchyard. Claverton Pumping Station (built 1809–13) pumps water from the river Avon up to the Kennet and Avon Canal to keep it topped up. It has been restored and is now an industrial heritage museum.

Claverton Manor (built for Sir Jeffry Wyatville in 1820) now houses the American Museum in Britain, which opened in 1961 (see p.73).

Much of Claverton Down is taken up by the campus of the University of Bath (see p.168). The area is also home to the headquarters of Wessex Water.

Combe Down and Odd Down: Incorporated into the city of Bath in the 1950s, Combe Down sits on a ridge to the south. The village was created in about 1729 by the entrepreneur Ralph Allen to house employees who worked in his nearby quarries. During the eighteenth and nineteenth centuries these quarries supplied huge amounts of Bath stone for the building of the city and for use farther afield. In 1738 Allen began building his mansion of Prior Park (now Prior Park College). In 1940 the Admiralty acquired a 46-acre (19-hectare) site, which was sold for housing in 2013.

Odd Down ('Odda's Hill') stands at the crossing point of two historical landmarks, the Wansdyke and the Fosse Way. It was also an area that had many stone quarries.

Bear Flat: Bear Flat lies on what was once the main pilgrimage route from Bath Abbey to the religious sites at Wells and Glastonbury. It stands on a short plateau (which may explain the 'flat' part of its name), and the 'bear' – no connection with the animal – is probably derived from '*bere*', the Saxon word for barley (hence 'beer').

Weston: Weston, as its name implies, lies to the (north) west of the city, and is made up of two parts: Upper and Lower Weston. The area has a long history, with evidence of occupation from Celtic times. In the medieval period it had close ties with the monks of Bath Abbey. The village expanded during the nineteenth century and has continued to grow. The church (All Saints) was completed in 1832, but there has been a church on this site since at least 1156. Bath's major hospital, the Royal United (or RUH), is located in Weston.

Lansdown: Its name (from Old English) means 'the long hill', and it lies to the north of Bath. Lansdown Hill was the site of the Battle of Lansdown in 1643 (see the section on 'Battles in and around Bath). On the top of the hill is the famous Bath Racecourse. It was on the steepest section of Lansdown Hill that, on a visit to the city in 1703, the coach in which Queen Anne was travelling began to slide backwards down the hill, due to the tiredness of the horses. Quick thinking by some of the servants, who put their shoulders to the wheels and stopped the coach by sheer force, prevented a serious accident. The Queen, we are told, was 'extremely frighted'.

Newbridge: This lies to the west between Bath and Bristol and is named after the New Bridge which spans the Avon and was built in 1734. It replaced a ford which needed to be removed when the Avon was made navigable between Bath and Bristol in 1727. Today it carries the A4. Partis College, a Grade I listed building on Newbridge Hill, was built between 1825 and 1827 as alms houses for women 'in reduced circumstances'. Today it still provides accommodation for women aged 50+ who are members of the Church of England.

Larkhall and Snow Hill: Described by the *Sunday Times* in 2015 as 'a trendy urban village', Larkhall lies to the north-east, with good views of Solsbury Hill. It began its development as a suburb in the early nineteenth century as a means of housing the ever-growing working population of Bath. Since 2007 there has been an annual community festival in May. The Larkhall Inn was established in 1784 in what was originally the Manor House. It became an important staging post for mail coaches on the old Gloucester Road.

Snow Hill is predominantly composed of terraced houses and flats from the 1950s. The most noticeable feature of the flats is their copper roofs, which have oxidised to a pale green. Copper was chosen as being a resilient and maintenance-free material. The area has a higher than average proportion of social housing.

Twerton: Twerton (formerly called Twiverton, meaning 'two ford town') is situated to the west of Bath. Its origins go back as far as the Domesday Book, but in the nineteenth century the village was demolished to make way for the Great Western Railway and was rebuilt close to the line. The novelist Henry Fielding once lived in Twerton and is thought to have written most of his famous novel *Tom Jones* there. Twerton is the home of Bath City Football Club.

4

BATH AT WORK

THEY BUILT BATH

The principal architects who helped to design the city we see today were:

John Wood the Elder (1704–54): He and his son are the most well-known of Bath's architects. Born near Bath, he began his career in Yorkshire, working for Lord Bingley, then returned to Bath with great plans to redevelop the city in the classical manner. He designed North and South Parades, Queen Square and The Circus, together with other buildings in the city. He died in the early stages of the building of The Circus.

John Wood the Younger (1728–82): He was born in the city and trained by his father. After the latter's death he completed The Circus, then went on to build the famous Royal Crescent and the upper Assembly Rooms in Brock Street. Outside of Bath, his best works include Buckland House in Oxfordshire and the General Infirmary in Salisbury, Wiltshire.

Robert Adam (1728–92): A Scottish architect, interior designer and furniture designer, Adam was at the forefront of the classical revival in England and Scotland, and was at one time MP for Kinross-shire. He designed Bath's famous Pulteney Bridge, which is the only example of his work to be found in the city.

Thomas Warr Attwood (1733–75): A plumber by trade, he acted as Bath's City Architect and Surveyor as well as having a seat on the City Council. Through his position he gained many lucrative contracts and commissions, including the new City Gaol. He was killed when a derelict building he was inspecting collapsed.

John Palmer (1738–1817): As City Architect and Surveyor, Palmer was responsible for Lansdown Crescent, St Swithin's church, Walcot, Christ church and the addition to the Royal Mineral Water Hospital (now the Royal National Hospital for Rheumatic Diseases). He should not be confused with the John Palmer (1742–1818), who was the theatre owner and mail coach pioneer, nor the twentieth-century fraudster and career criminal of the same name.

Thomas Baldwin (1750–1820): From 1775 to 1800 he was the City Architect and Surveyor for Bath, and was responsible for designing many of its public buildings, including the Guildhall, Great Pulteney Street, Laura Place and the Grand Pump Room Hotel (now demolished).

John Eveleigh (dates unknown): Began working in Bath in the 1780s, and was responsible for Camden Crescent (1788), Beaufort Buildings (1790) and Somerset Place (1791). He went bankrupt when the City Bank failed in 1793, and he moved to Plymouth.

John Pinch the Elder (1769–1827): A Cornishman by birth, he succeeded Thomas Baldwin as Bath's Surveyor and was responsible for many of the later Georgian buildings in the city. His achievements include Cavendish Place and Crescent, St Mary's, Bathwick and Sion Hill Place. His son, John Pinch the Younger (1796–1849), worked in partnership with his father, and together they carried out a number of commissions in Bathwick. The younger Pinch later worked on redesigning some of the west side of Queen Square.

Major Charles Edward Davis (1827–1902): He worked on the excavation and redevelopment of the Roman Baths in the 1870s and '80s, but his work met with strong criticism on archaeological grounds and he was not allowed to complete the work. He went on to design the Empire Hotel (1901) in Orange Grove, a building which, even today, arouses fierce controversy, and is sometimes referred to as 'Major Davis's Revenge'! His title of 'Major' came from the commission he had held with the Worcestershire Militia.

INDUSTRY IN BATH

The firm of Stothert and Pitt was founded in the city in 1785. They produced a whole range of products, including cranes, engineering plant and cast-iron household items. The company was founded by George Stothert, who was later joined by Robert Pitt. By 1815 they had their own foundry and exhibited at the Great Exhibition of 1851. They specialised in dockside and bulk-handling cranes and they also worked on tank design in the Second World War. They were a major employer in the city; in 1945 more than 2,000 people worked for them. In 1989 the company failed, owing to the collapse of the Maxwell empire, to whom the business had been sold three years earlier. However, examples of their products can still be seen around the country, such as their Fairbairn steam crane on the harbourside at Bristol.

The company known as J.B. Bowler was founded in 1872 by Jonathan Burdett Bowler, a Victorian entrepreneur who set up an engineering business. A self-made man, Bowler described himself as a 'brass founder, engineer, gas fitter, locksmith and bell hanger', and visited his customers on a bicycle. The company also manufactured and sold fizzy drinks with such evocative names as Cherry Ciderette, Orange Champagne, Bath Punch and Hot Tom. The company continued through several generations of the family, finally closing in 1969, when the founder's grandson retired. The factory has been carefully recreated at The Museum of Bath at Work in Julian Road.

Gustav Horstmann (1828–93) was a German clockmaker who designed the world's first micrometer that was accurate to one ten-thousandth of an inch, and also pioneered the self-winding clock. Gustav's son Sidney formed the Horstmann company in 1913, and they became pioneers in the automotive industry, producing cars which were successfully raced at Brooklands. During the First World War, accusations that the company was a German one, and therefore disloyal to England, led Sidney eventually to drop the final 'n' from the car-making side of the business (although retaining it for the gear and switch making operations).

Rotork Ltd is a company that manufactures valves, gearboxes, control systems and other accessories. Although it began life in Bristol in the 1940s, it moved to Bath in 1957. At first it operated from Widcombe Manor, then moved to new premises at Newbridge in 1967, where it is still based. Over the years Rotork has acquired a number of other companies in Europe and the United States. The company is now a market leader in flow-control products and is registered on the FTSE Index.

The Pitman Press (which later changed its name to the Bath Press) developed from the Phonetic Institute founded by Sir Isaac Pitman, of shorthand fame, in 1899, and was located on the Lower Bristol Road. The business was considerably extended over subsequent years, and continued to flourish under the leadership of Sir Isaac's sons and grandsons. One of the grandsons, Sir James Pitman, was responsible for creating the Initial Teaching Alphabet, which became popular in many schools during the 1960s and '70s. The Bath Press closed in 2007, with the site earmarked for housing.

Archaeologists excavating in Sawclose prior to the commencement of work on the building of a new casino and hotel, discovered an eighteenth-century clay tobacco pipe factory. Pipe-making in Bath started in the 1650s, with clay being brought from Devon, using the river Avon. The pipes were fired in kilns, of which several almost complete examples have been found. For the first forty years of the eighteenth century pipe-making in Bath was dominated by the Carpenter family; in the nineteenth century the Sants family became pre-eminent and they took over the Sawclose factory in 1836. The factory was demolished in 1859 when the renewal of its lease was refused on the grounds of pollution.

The quarrying of Bath stone is dealt with in a separate chapter.

LONG-ESTABLISHED AND SPECIALIST SHOPS

Here are a few of the businesses which are (or were) unique to Bath or have a long association with the city:

Paxton and Whitfield, John Street is a specialist cheese shop and Britain's leading cheesemonger for over 200 years, holding two Royal Warrants. They also sell wines and other foods such as hams, biscuits and preserves, and supply cheeses to the restaurant trade throughout the south-west. Sir Winston Churchill is quoted as saying: 'A gentleman only buys his cheese from Paxton and Whitfield'.

Jolly's, Milsom Street was founded by father and son James and Thomas Jolly, who came to Bath in 1823. They first opened a store in Old Bond Street and later moved to Milsom Street, where their store became known as the 'Bath Emporium', a department store selling a wide range of products. In 1968 the company was acquired by Dingle & Co. of Plymouth, who were themselves taken over in 1971 by House of Fraser.

Bayntun's, in Manvers Street, was established in 1894 by George Bayntun, and in 1939 it acquired the bookbinding business of Robert Riviere, which had been established in 1829. It is the last of the family owned Victorian trade binderies and continues to use traditional, hand-crafted techniques. It also specialises in secondhand and rare books and antique prints.

Mallory, the jewellers in Bridge Street, has been a family-owned business for over 100 years. It was started in 1898 by Edward Palmer Mallory and his wife and soon gained a reputation as Bath's premier jewellery shop. They also made watches for the Admiralty, as a sign outside the shop proclaims.

The Thermae Bath Spa Shop, Hot Bath Street, is located opposite the main entrance to the Spa complex. This shop offers a selection of spa gifts, together with a whole range of health and beauty products, some of which are produced using the natural thermal spring water.

Cater, Stoffell and Fortt was a Bath grocery firm founded in the nineteenth century by Richard Bryant Cater and grew to become one of the city's most successful retail businesses. They specialised in high-class catering, grocery, confectionery, wines and spirits, and also produced the well-known Bath Oliver biscuits. The company ceased trading in the 1970s.

MARKETS IN BATH

Bath has several popular markets catering for all tastes. Here are some of them:

The Guildhall Market (High Street) has operated from its current site since the sixteenth century – although there has been a market in Bath for about 800 years. The present building was completed in the 1770s and the dome was added in 1863. The earlier market was held at the old street level, underneath the vaults that now support Grand Parade. Today, the market contains fruit and vegetable stalls, butchers, fishmongers, a secondhand bookstall and many other traders, and still has a very traditional feel. It is open every day (except Sunday). An unusual feature of this market is that it contains a 'nail'; an eighteenth-century stone pillar or table on which transactions were once carried out and payment made. This is said to have given rise to the expression 'to pay on the nail'.

Bath Farmers' Market (Green Park Station) is held every Saturday between 9.30 a.m. and 12.30 p.m. in what was once the Bath terminus of the Midland and the Somerset and Dorset Railways. Almost all of the produce is sourced from within a 40-mile radius of Bath and sold by the people who produce it. Get there early for the maximum amount of choice!

Bath Artisan Market (Green Park Station) is an independent, award-winning market with vintage and handmade art, gourmet food and a craft workshop. This covered market specialises in goods that are ethical, locally made and original. It is held on the second Sunday of every month, from 10 a.m. until 4 p.m.

Bath Flea Market (Bath Racecourse, Lansdown) has around 250 stalls, selling 'vintage, antique, shabby-chic and unique' items. It is held monthly, but on different days.

Bath Christmas Market, perhaps Bath's most famous market, is a German-style Christmas Market held in and around Abbey Churchyard. The wooden chalet-type stalls sell high-quality artisan products, including food and gifts, many of which are locally produced. The market was started in 2002 and due to its popularity has expanded each year since. It is open every day from late November to mid-December and runs for a period of about eighteen days.

OCCUPATIONS IN VICTORIAN BATH

The following list shows the occupations of residents of No. 1 Abbey Street (then a common lodging-house) between 1841 and 1901.*

Attendant at Baths
Blacksmith
Bookseller
Caretaker
Chairman (i.e., Bath Chair attendant)
Charwoman
Coal miner
Dairyman
Dressmaker
Errand boy
Family servant
Fly (carriage) proprietor
Foreman of Gas Company
French polisher
Housemaid
Labourer
Laundress
Living on Means
Mason
Musician
Needlewoman
Nurse
Pauper
Porter
Printer
Schoolmistress
Seamstress

Shoemaker's apprentice
Shop assistant
Stay maker
Tailor
Umbrella maker
Upholsterer
Waiter
Waitress

* Information taken from Census records

AN INTERESTING IDEA, BUT ...

In 2007 the UK's first 'therapeutic salt cave' opened in a house in James Street West. Using salt crystals from their native Poland, the owners hoped that the attraction would prove beneficial to people with respiratory complaints, who would breathe the salt-laden air to the accompaniment of soothing music. Unfortunately, after a promising start, the project proved commercially non-viable and the business closed after only one year.

Self-styled doctor James Graham set up a practice in Bath in 1778, where he promoted the virtues of his electro-magnetic 'Celestial Bed', which, it was claimed, would give couples the best chance of conceiving. He also promoted various other 'cures', one of which, 'earth-bathing', involved being buried in the ground up to the neck. Not surprisingly, he eventually ran into debt, and his mental health suffered. He died in Edinburgh in 1794.

Ronald 'Ron' Clark came to Bath in the 1970s with the aim of promoting an International Auxiliary Language of his own devising, which became known as 'Glosa'. This was based on an earlier attempt by Lancelot Hogben, which he had called 'Interglossa'. Together with Wendy Ashby, Clark promoted the language, which, it was claimed, took only 20 hours to learn, with a dictionary comprising 1,700 words. However, like other 'artificial' languages such as Esperanto, its speakers tend to remain in a very small minority.

In 1965 the Traffic Consultant to Bath Corporation, Professor Colin Buchanan, suggested that, in order to alleviate Bath's traffic problems, a tunnel should be dug beneath the city. The tunnel was to be 590 yards (540m) long and 20ft (6m) below the city centre, and would have a dual carriageway. The scheme met with fierce opposition from some quarters and was eventually deemed to be too expensive. The idea was finally abandoned in 1979.

5

CULTURAL AND LITERARY BATH

ALL THE WORLD'S A STAGE

The Theatre Royal, Sawclose, has had its share of successes and failures since it opened on 12 October 1805.

The first play to be staged was Shakespeare's *King Richard III*, and, for reasons which have never become clear, the title role was played by 'a Young Gentleman; His First Appearance on any Stage'. Although he had apparently performed well in rehearsals, on the opening night he fell prey to severe stage fright, forgetting his words, and the evening was a disaster. By a curious coincidence, on 19 October 1741 a production of the same play at the theatre in Goodman's Fields in London had seen the title role taken by 'a Gentleman who never appeared on any Stage'. This opening night had a much happier ending, however, as the 'gentleman' in question was the young David Garrick, who went on to become a theatrical superstar.

Sir Henry Irving, hailed as the greatest actor of his time, first trod the boards of the Theatre Royal in September 1867, appearing in two of Richard Brinsley Sheridan's plays: *The Rivals* and *The School for Scandal*. He returned to Bath four years later in Albery's *The Two Roses*. Irving was responsible for several theatrical innovations, including introducing the darkening of the auditorium during performances and the closing of the curtains between scenes; prior to this, scene-shifting had taken place in full view of the audience.

On Good Friday 1862 the interior of the theatre was destroyed by fire, the cause of which was never satisfactorily explained. Unfortunately, the theatre had been insured for only £4,000 – half the cost of rebuilding. Subscriptions were raised, and the restored theatre opened, with a performance of *A Midsummer Night's Dream*, in March 1863.

During the performance of a play in 1963 a clock, which was being used as a stage prop and had no mechanism, suddenly chimed three times, despite its hands having been set to 12.30. At the same time the stage lights dimmed. No explanation has ever been found.

The great French tragedienne Sarah Bernhardt appeared on the Bath stage in 1916, despite being 72 years old and having had a leg amputated. She played the part of a mortally wounded French soldier (she specialised in playing male roles).

The crimson stage curtains were endowed by Lady Oona Chaplin, wife of Sir Charles (Charlie). His intertwined initials can be seen embroidered on them in gold thread.

By the 1970s the theatre was badly in need of restoration and its future was in doubt. £2 million was needed; an appeal was launched, but initially fell far short of the target. However, thanks to support from various banks, building societies and county councils, the necessary amount was raised and the theatre reopened in November 1982 – again with a performance of Shakespeare's *'Dream'*.

IT'LL BE ALL RIGHT ON THE NIGHT

Famous actors who have performed in Bath:

John Henderson (1747–85): Known as 'the Bath Roscius' (a famous Roman actor), he was the rival and successor to David Garrick and greatly admired for his interpretations of Shakespearean roles.

Sir Henry Irving (1838–1905): The first actor to receive a knighthood. He first played at the Bath Theatre Royal in 1867. In 1902 he unveiled the plaque to James Quin outside Quin's Bath address in Pierrepont Street.

Edmund Kean (1787–1833): Regarded in his time as the greatest Shakespearean actor ever. His last words were said to have been 'dying is easy; comedy is hard'.

James Quin (1693–1766): Irish actor famous for his portrayal of Shakespeare's Sir John Falstaff. He retired to Bath, which he called 'a fine slope to the grave'. He is buried in the abbey, where he has an epitaph composed by fellow actor David Garrick.

Mrs Sarah Siddons (1755–1831): The most acclaimed female actor of her generation, famous for her role as Lady Macbeth. She played at the old Theatre Royal, Orchard Street.

Dame Ellen Terry (1847–1928): First appeared on the Bath stage, in the role of Titania, in 1863 at the age of 16, and went on to become the leading female Shakespearean actor of her generation, with a career that spanned seven decades. Her grand-nephew was the actor Sir John Gielgud, who played the Theatre Royal in the 1940s.

Famous stage, film and television actors who have played at Bath's Theatre Royal in more recent times include (among many others): Stewart Granger, Charlton Heston, Richard Todd, Dame Anna Neagle, Sir Ian McKellen, Sir Patrick Stewart, Dame Maggie Smith, Lauren Bacall, Sir Anthony Hopkins, Felicity Kendal, Vanessa Redgrave and Dame Joan Collins.

In a small courtyard just off Sawclose is a raised plant bed, around the edge of which are palm prints from the hands of sixteen famous celebrities of the stage and screen, including Peter Ustinov, Joan Collins, Derek Jacobi and Maureen Lipman.

PIONEERS OF THE SILVER SCREEN

Bristol-born William Friese-Greene is regarded by many as the true inventor of cinematography. He came to Bath in the early 1870s as an assistant at a photographic studio. He soon opened his own premises in Gay Street and then the Corridor. Fascinated by the idea of moving pictures, he began experimenting with various techniques, and in 1890 he filed a patent for his apparatus, which he demonstrated to the Bath Photographic Society the same year. He moved to London, where he filed more than seventy more patents, but made little money, and at the time of his death in 1929 he was impoverished. His tomb is in Highgate Cemetery, London. His grandson was the actor Richard Greene, famous for his portrayal of Robin Hood.

While in Bath, Friese-Greene had come into contact with John Arthur Roebuck Rudge, a Bath-born inventor and scientific instrument maker, and the two men collaborated in the development of cinematic apparatus. In 1875 Rudge invented the Rudge Projector, or Biophantascope, a forerunner of the modern cine projector, which showed a number of slides in quick succession, giving the illusion of movement. Rudge lived in New Bond Street Place, where plaques in memory of both men can be seen.

LOCATION, LOCATION

Bath has become a popular venue for film companies. These are some of the films and television programmes that have used the city as a location:

The Titfield Thunderbolt (1953), an Ealing comedy starring Stanley Holloway and John Gregson, was filmed in Monkton Combe, just outside the city.

Persuasion (1971) starring Anne Firbank and Bryan Marshall); (1995) starring Amanda Root and Ciaran Hinds and (2007) starring Alice Hawkins and Rupert Penry-Jones – scenes for all these television productions of Jane Austen's celebrated novel were filmed at various locations in the city.

Joseph Andrews (1977), starring Peter Firth and Ann-Margret, an adaption of Henry Fielding's novel, was partly filmed at the Roman Baths and the Royal Crescent.

Agatha (1979), starring Vanessa Redgrave and Dustin Hoffman, a fictional account of the real-life eleven days' disappearance of Agatha Christie in 1926, used Bath as a stand-in for 1920s Harrogate.

Northanger Abbey (1987) starring Katharine Schlesinger and Peter Firth, another of Jane Austen's novels, was filmed at the Assembly Rooms. The 2007 version with Felicity Jones and J.J. Field, however, was filmed entirely in Ireland.

Buffalo Girls (1995), starring Anjelica Huston and Sam Elliott, a made-for-television film with a Western theme had scenes filmed in Queen Street.

Pie in the Sky (1995), the popular detective/restaurateur series starring Richard Griffiths and Maggie Steed, had an episode entitled 'Swan in his Pride' set in Bath.

The Hollow Reed (1996), starring Joely Richardson and Martin Donovan, was concerned with domestic abuse, and was filmed at various locations in the city.

Inspector Morse (1997), the hugely successful television series that ran from 1987 until 2000, starring John Thaw and Kevin Whately, was mainly set in Oxford. However, the episode 'Death is now my Neighbour' (season 10), included scenes shot in the Royal Crescent and The Circus.

Vanity Fair (2004), for this production of Thackeray's famous novel, starring Reese Witherspoon and Gabriel Byrne, Great Pulteney Street doubled as Great Curzon Street in London. The replica gas lamps now lining the street were a gift from the film company.

Beau Brummell: This Charming Man (2006) starring James Purefoy and Hugh Bonneville was a made-for-television film depicting the life of the notorious Regency dandy. Scenes were filmed at North Parade Buildings.

Dracula (2006), a television movie retelling Bram Stoker's famous vampire story, starring David Suchet and Marc Warren, had scenes filmed at Abbey Green.

The Duchess (2007) starring Keira Knightley and Ralph Fiennes, chronicled the exploits of Georgiana, the eighteenth-century Duchess of Devonshire. Scenes were filmed in the Assembly Rooms.

Bonekickers (2008), an ill-fated television series starring Julie Graham and Hugh Bonneville, featured a team of archaeologists solving historical mysteries. Locations included the Roman Baths, Kingston Parade and the Assembly Rooms. It was poorly received and ran for only one series.

Les Misérables (2012), starring Hugh Jackman and Russell Crowe, had Pulteney Weir as the location for the suicide of Inspector Javert (Crowe), with the Avon doubling as the Seine.

Unknown Heart (2013), a television film based on a Rosamunde Pilcher novel starring Jane Seymour and Julian Sands, had scenes filmed in the Royal Crescent.

Sherlock (2015) starring Benedict Cumberbatch and Martin Freeman, had the 2015 Christmas special, 'The Abominable Bride', filmed in the Queen Street/Trim Street area of the city.

MUSICAL BATH

The world-famous violinist Yehudi Menuhin served as Musical Director to the Bath International Music Festival from 1959 to 1969. During that time he and his family frequently stayed at the Lansdown Grove Hotel.

'Grammy' winner James 'Midge' Ure, of Ultravox and Band Aid fame, lives on the outskirts of Bath and has supported many worthwhile causes in the city.

Singer/songwriter Peter Gabriel has a home in the nearby village of Box, where he owns a recording studio named Real World. His composition 'Solsbury Hill' was inspired by the Bath location.

Irish singer and musician George 'Van' Morrison once had a home in the Lansdown area of the city and recorded several of his albums in or near Bath.

Roland Orzabal and Curt Smith met when they were pupils at Beechen Cliff School and went on to form Tears for Fears, one of the most notable 'new wave' bands of the 1980s.

Another eighties band, The Korgis, were performing at Mole's, a venue in central Bath, when they attracted the attention of record label scouts. They released their first album in 1979.

Jazz vocalist and musician Jamie Cullum regularly visits Bath, where his parents live. At a charity concert in the city in 2005 he played to more than 6,000 people.

Pianist, composer and conductor Alberto Semprini was born in Bath. He hosted a light music programme on BBC radio for twenty-five years and also became a popular figure on television.

The conductor and harpsichordist Raymond Leppard grew up in Bath, where he attended what is now Beechen Cliff School. He achieved international fame as a conductor and has been influential in encouraging the revival of interest in baroque music.

Venanzio Rauzzini (1746–1810) was a composer, singer, pianist and concert impresario. Born in Italy, he settled in Bath in 1780, where he became Director of Concerts at the New Assembly Rooms. He was a friend of Joseph Haydn, who often stayed with him. Rauzzini is buried in Bath Abbey, where there is a plaque commemorating him. As a castrato he was able to achieve very high notes, and the motet 'Exultate Jubilate' was specially composed for him by Mozart.

MUSEUMS AND GALLERIES

Some of the most popular museums and collections in the city:

The Roman Baths Museum (Abbey Churchyard): One of Britain's major visitor attractions, the Roman Baths complex is located on the site of the largest of Bath's geothermal springs. Built and enlarged between the first and fourth centuries AD, they form the most complete suite of Roman baths in northern Europe. The journey through the museum takes the visitor down to the old Roman street level, about 16ft (5m) below that of the present-day. As well as audio guides and video presentations there are also live actors who will interact with visitors. Disability access is excellent and entry is through a nineteenth-century concert hall. There is a charge for admission.

The Holburne Museum (Sydney Place): Housed in a building that dates from 1799 and was formerly the Sydney Hotel, the museum stands in its own grounds. It houses a collection of fine and decorative art and includes works by Gainsborough, Stubbs and Zoffany. This was originally built around the collection of Sir Thomas Holburne (1793–1874), a Scottish baronet. The museum runs a programme of lectures, workshops and temporary exhibitions, and there is a bookshop and a café. A new £11.2 million extension was opened in 2011. Entry is free, but temporary exhibitions usually carry a charge.

The Victoria Art Gallery (Broad Street): Opened in 1897, the year of Queen Victoria's Diamond Jubilee, it houses a large collection of paintings, sculpture and decorative arts. Paintings include works by Gainsborough, Sickert and Lawrence, and the collection contains examples from the fifteenth century to the present day. Admission is free, but there is sometimes a charge for temporary exhibitions.

The Museum of Bath Architecture (formerly The Building of Bath Collection) (The Paragon): This is housed in the former Countess of Huntingdon's Chapel and tells the story of the building of the city during the eighteenth century. Owned and run by the Bath Preservation Trust, the museum contains models, drawings, maps and reconstructions, showing exactly how a Georgian house was constructed, furnished and decorated. There is an admission charge.

The Assembly Rooms and Fashion Museum (Bennett Street): Originally known as the 'New' or 'Upper' Rooms, they were designed by the younger John Wood and opened in 1771 to serve the fashionable area that included The Circus and the Royal Crescent. Here, visitors could dance, play cards, take tea and mingle with the high society of the city. Grand Balls were held at least twice a week during the Bath Season. Today the rooms are used for weddings, concerts, exhibitions etc. They are owned by the National Trust and operated by Bath and North East Somerset Council. There is free admission to the rooms.

The Fashion Museum (formerly known as the Museum of Costume) is located in the basement and focuses on fashionable clothing from the 1600s to the present day. The collection has over 30,000 objects. Every year the 'Dress of the Year', by famous designers such as Versace, is featured, and there are regular special exhibitions. There is a charge for the museum (unless you are a Bath resident with a Discovery Card), but you can buy joint discount tickets with the Roman Baths or No. 1 Royal Crescent.

No. 1 Royal Crescent: Comprising thirty houses, the Crescent was completed in 1775, and was the work of the younger Wood, although the original idea had been his father's. Since then it has been Bath's most exclusive address, with the houses originally being built to be let by their owners during the 'Season'. No. 1, an exceptionally fine example of a Georgian town house, was given to Bath Preservation Trust in 1968, and, after restoration, was opened to the public in 1970. A visit to the house takes you into the world of Henry Sandford, the first resident. There is a charge for admission.

Bath Postal Museum (Northgate Street): It was at Bath that the world's first postage stamp was issued in May 1840. This museum was founded in 1979 and traces the history of postal services in Britain from early times to the present, with many artefacts and lots of archive material. There is a charge for admission.

The American Museum in Britain (Claverton Manor): The only museum of its kind outside the USA, it tells the story of American cultural history. The 1820s house, set in 120 acres of parkland, contains many period rooms and exhibitions of folk and decorative arts, as well as the popular Orangery Café. Do you know what a 'snickerdoodle' is? Well, you can find out here! There is a charge for admission.

Herschel Museum of Astronomy (New King Street): Located in the former home of William Herschel (1738–1832), the German-born astronomer and discoverer of the planet Uranus in 1781, this restored Georgian house contains many items relating to the family. You can see the family music room, Herschel's workshop and the garden from which he made his famous discovery. There are also occasional temporary exhibitions. There is a charge for admission.

Museum of Bath at Work (Julian Road): This is housed in an eighteenth-century Real Tennis court and traces Bath's development as a manufacturing and retail centre. The centrepiece of the museum is a reconstruction of the soft drinks and engineering works of Jonathan Burdett Bowler, a Victorian engineer and businessman (see p.56). Other floors contain masses of artefacts and curiosities, including photographs, sound recordings and films. There is a charge for admission.

The Museum of East Asian Art: This is located in Bennett Street and is the only museum in the country specifically dedicated to the cultures of east and south-east Asia. It contains some exhibits that go back 7,000 years. There is a charge for admission.

Bath also has its own 'Virtual Museum', www.bathnewseum.com; an online forum which was started by former local radio and television presenter Richard Wyatt. This is intended as a 'living' museum of the city's history and heritage, to which anyone may contribute items of interest.

FESTIVALS IN BATH

Bath plays host to many festivals and events during the year, such as:

Bath International Music Festival: This takes place in late May/ early June every year. Started in 1948, it includes a variety of music, such as orchestral, jazz, folk, electronic and world music. Many top musicians have taken part over the years and Yehudi Menuhin was its artistic director from 1959 until 1968. The festival also runs non-musical events such as talks. Events take place at various locations throughout the city.

The Bath Fringe Festival: Since 1981 this has run concurrently with the Music Festival. It is aimed at a younger audience and seeks to provide a contrast to the classically dominated IMF, which was perceived by some as elitist.

The Jane Austen Festival: This is a festival devoted to Jane, her life and works. It was started in 2001 and takes place over a ten-day period in October each year. There are various events each day, including themed walks led by local guides, concerts, talks, workshops and a grand Promenade of people dressed in period costume.

The Bath Mozartfest: A festival devoted to the great composer and some of his contemporaries. Held each November for over twenty years, the performances are given by some of the foremost names in classical music.

The Bath Literature Festival: The festival was started in 1995 and is held in February/March each year at various venues in the city. It is sponsored by the *Independent* newspaper. Previous speakers have included P.D. James, J.K. Rowling, Terry Pratchett and Alexander McCall Smith. There is also a Festival of Children's Literature, sponsored by the *Telegraph* newspaper and held each year in September/October.

The Great Bath Feast: A food festival that lasts for the month of October, with a huge range of different food and drink and demonstrations by top chefs. It's run in conjunction with some of Bath's premier restaurants and attracts a large following each year (very large, in some cases!).

The Bath Comedy Festival: This includes comedy shows, cabarets, music and a host of other events at different locations. Held in March/April, former guest artists have included such stalwarts as Barry Cryer and Arthur Smith.

Bath Film Festival: Held in November each year, at various locations, it features previews, documentaries, family films, discussions and debates. Its patron is film and television director Ken Loach.

ARTISTS OF BATH

In the past, a number of famous painters made their homes in Bath, drawn by the picturesque location as well as the fact that many wealthy visitors would pay to have their portraits painted, just as today they might pose for a photograph.

Peter Brown (b. 1967): Known as 'Pete the Street', he is an impressionist painter who has made his home in Bath. His speciality is landscapes and street scenes and he always paints on location. He is a member of the New English Art Club and became the first Artist in Residence at the Savoy Hotel, London. Examples of his work are regularly on show at the Victoria Art Gallery, Bath.

Benjamin Barker (1776–1838): Benjamin was the younger brother of Thomas Barker and specialised in watercolour views and landscapes. He lived for a while in Bathwick Street, then built himself a house on Bathwick Hill, where Queen Charlotte is said to have visited him. Although gifted, he never achieved the success enjoyed by his brother. He died at Totnes, Devon, after a long illness.

Thomas Barker (1769–1847): Born in South Wales, he (like Gainsborough) showed early artistic talent and was entirely self-taught. The family moved to Bath when he was sixteen, and he became the protégé of a wealthy coachbuilder named Charles Spackman, who encouraged him to develop his talents. Spackman sent him to Rome to study and, on his return, Barker built up an extremely successful career

painting mostly landscapes, becoming known as 'Barker of Bath'. He became very wealthy and built himself a house in Cavendish Road (the 'Doric House'), which may be seen today.

Thomas Gainsborough (1727–88): He was born in Sudbury, Suffolk, and showed an early aptitude for painting and drawing. In 1759 he moved, together with his wife and children, to Bath, where he took up residence at No. 17 The Circus. He had one of the windows enlarged to provide more light to his studio. Some of his finest work was produced here, including his famous 'Blue Boy'. He soon acquired a reputation as an exceptional painter of portraits of the famous (and notorious), and became one of the earliest members of the Royal Society of Arts. He moved to London in 1774, where he became the royal family's favourite painter. He died in 1788 and is buried at Kew.

William Hoare (1707–92): He was the foremost painter of portraits in Bath prior to the arrival of Gainsborough. His famous portrait of Beau Nash hangs in the Sun Lounge of the Pump Room and there is a memorial to him in the abbey. He was a founder member of the Royal Academy. His son, Prince Hoare (1755–1834), was named after William's brother, and became a well-known painter and dramatist.

Sir Thomas Lawrence (1769–1830): Lawrence was born in Bristol, but when he was 4 his family moved to Devizes, Wiltshire, where his father became landlord of the Black Bear (now the Bear Hotel), a coaching inn. During their time there young Thomas showed a precocious talent for drawing and would often produce portraits of the customers. In 1780 the Lawrences moved to Bath, taking up residence at No. 2 Alfred Street, where young Thomas's income was already enough to support the family. At 18 Thomas left Bath for London, where he became a student at the Royal Academy and eventually its president. He was knighted in 1815 and died, probably from heart disease, in 1830. He is buried in St Paul's Cathedral, London.

STILL AS A STATUE

Some of the statues and sculptures, old and new, which can be seen on a walk around Bath.

Standing in a niche high on the wall of the Victoria Art Gallery, is a statue of Queen Victoria by the Anglo–Italian sculptor Andrea Carlo Lucchesi (d. 1925). The building was opened in 1897 to mark the 60th anniversary of Victoria's accession.

In the Parade Gardens there is a statue of a young Wolfgang Amadeus Mozart playing the violin. It was created by David Backhouse and unveiled in 1991.

The lead Scales of Justice statue stands above the pediment on the Guildhall, High Street. She holds the scales and sword of justice, but does not wear a blindfold. The building was opened in 1778.

The marble statue of Rebecca at the Well stands on the fountain on the north side of Bath Abbey. It was erected by the Bath Temperance Society in 1861 and carries the inscription 'Water is Best'. The statue and fountain were cleaned and restored by a team of students from Bath City College in 2013.

A statue of King Bladud, legendary founder of Bath, stands in Parade Gardens. It was carved in 1859 by Stefano Valerio Pieroni and once adorned the top of a public fountain that formerly stood in Bath Street. Accompanying Bladud is a modern stone pig, sculpted by Nigel Bryant and City of Bath College students. Another statue of Bladud, thought to be medieval, can be seen overlooking the King's Bath.

The Angel of Peace, or King Edward VII Memorial, can be seen near the foot of the steps by the entrance to Parade Gardens. The sculptor was Newbury Abbot Trent and the statue formerly stood in George Street. King Edward occupied the throne from 1901 to 1910 and his reign is commemorated on a bronze plaque beneath the statue.

Two lions stand on top of the gates leading into the western (Queen's Gate) entrance of Royal Victoria Park. Each has a paw resting on a ball. Placed in position in 1832, they look as though they are made from bronze, but are actually composed of Coade stone, an artificial stone created by Eleanor Coade in the eighteenth century. Bath children are sometimes teased that these lions descend at night to prowl the park. There are actually more than 500 representations of lions around the city.

Also in Victoria Park, opposite the Botanical Gardens, can be seen a large bust of the Roman god Jupiter, which weighs 6 tons. It was carved in about 1835 by John Osborne, a mason/sculptor who died in poverty in 1838.

Two statues can be seen in niches on the narrow building in Bath Street, next to the entrance to the Thermae Spa. These statues are believed to date from the fifteenth century, and to have once stood on the façade of Inigo Jones's original Town Hall of 1625. But – who are they? Opinions seem divided, with some sources claiming that they represent King Edgar (on the right, in armour) and King Cole. Others (including Sir Nikolaus Pevsner) maintain that the figure on the left is meant to represent the Anglo-Saxon King Osric (claimed as the founder of Bath Abbey). Who knows for certain?

The Resurrected Christ, at the south-east corner of Bath Abbey was created on site by local sculptor Lawrence Tindall for the Bath Abbey 2000 celebrations. The statue shows Jesus bursting the bonds of death and is carved from local Bath stone.

The chubby cherub who stands in an alcove in the side of a shop at the end of Old Bond Street was once part of the Melfort Cross. This once stood in the centre of the Cross Bath (giving it its name), and is said to commemorate the visit to Bath in 1687 of Mary of Modena, wife of King James II, who had come to take the waters in the hope of producing an heir.

The statues which stand on the terrace of the Roman Baths are not (as some people imagine) Roman. Most are Victorian, while one (that of Julius Caesar) is even more modern, having been carved in the 1980s to replace the earlier one which was destroyed by vandals. All are male (except for the bust of Roma, the female deity who personified the city of Rome), and represent important figures from Romano–British history, including some emperors and governors of Britain.

On the façade of the west tunnel, which carries the Kennet and Avon Canal through Sydney Gardens, can be seen the carved head of Sabrina, the Roman personification of the river Severn. Facing her, on the entrance to the west tunnel, is the head of Father Thames. One end of the canal links with the Thames via the river Kennet, while the other is linked to the Severn by the river Avon.

On a high wall in Walcot Street can be seen more than thirty grotesque faces carved in Bath stone; some mystical or comical, others representing local people. This display was begun in the 1980s and has been added to more recently. The display is part of an art project aimed at encouraging visitors to the artisan quarter of the city. The sculptor who carved the original faces was Paul Rogers; the more recent (2013) ones are the work of Pete Bloomfield.

On the face of the nearby Podium is a frieze showing a number of figures, including Prince Bladud, a Roman soldier, a Georgian man, Victorian and Edwardian ladies and a modern busker. The sculptor was Barry Baldwin from nearby Corsham.

The north wing of the Guildhall also carries a stone frieze. The figures here represent a variety of trades and activities, including engineering, physics, chemistry, navigation, architecture, music, painting and others. This part of the Guildhall once housed a technical college.

The West Front of Bath Abbey contains a wealth of sculpture – in fact, a huge picture in stone. Prominent among them are the angels ascending (and descending) ladders between earth and heaven. The upside-down ones are, presumably, coming down – how else do you illustrate the difference in a carving? Also seen are Christ in Majesty, the Heavenly Host (much eroded), the Dove of Peace, the Apostles and King Henry VII, during whose reign the abbey was begun. On the buttresses at either side is the rebus, or word picture, of the name of Bishop Oliver King, who was the moving force behind the rebuilding of the abbey in 1499 (see p.110).

In the tympanum of the pediment above the nineteenth-century extension to the Mineral Water Hospital is a representation of the parable of the Good Samaritan. To the left, in the pediment of John Wood's original building can be seen the Royal Arms of George II.

A life-sized sculpture representing the swimmer Mark Foster, Olympic and Commonwealth Games medal winner, can be seen outside the City of Bath College. The sculptor is Bath-based Ben Dearnley.

LITERARY BATH

Among the famous authors who have resided in or visited the city, are:

Jane Austen (1775–1817): She had several addresses in the city; firstly at No. 4 Sydney Place from 1801 to 1805, then in Green Park Buildings and finally Gay Street, before moving out of Bath. She also stayed for a few weeks at No. 13 Queen Square, and with her aunt and uncle at No. 1 The Paragon. Two of her works, *Northanger Abbey* and *Persuasion*, feature Bath prominently, though the city gets a mention in all her novels.

Frances 'Fanny' Burney (1752–1840): Novelist, diarist and playwright; her first and most famous novel was *Evelina*, published anonymously in 1778 to critical acclaim. She was also a prolific writer of journals and letters, which she began writing at the age of 15. On her arrival in Bath she stayed with her friend Hester Thrale at No. 14 South Parade.

Charles Dickens (1812–70): He first came to Bath as a young Parliamentary reporter, staying at the Saracen's Head Inn in Broad Street. While there he was working on his first novel, the famous *Pickwick Papers*, which was published in 1836. The name of the leading character was inspired by the Pickwick family of Bath, who ran a local coaching company. Dickens later stayed on a number of occasions with his friend Walter Savage Landor at No. 35 St James's Square.

Henry Fielding (1707–54): Novelist and dramatist, he is most famous for his novel *Tom Jones* (1749). He lived with his sister Sarah in the Lodge at Widcombe, a village which is now part of the city. He was also a frequent guest at nearby Prior Park Mansion.

Oliver Goldsmith (1728–74): Playwright, poet and novelist, author of works such as *She Stoops to Conquer* and *The Vicar of Wakefield*, as well as a biography of Beau Nash, he stayed at No. 11 North Parade when he came to Bath in 1771.

Dr Samuel Johnson (1709–84): The essayist and compiler of the famous Dictionary came to Bath in 1766 and lodged at the Pelican Inn (since demolished) in Walcot Street. His biography, by James Boswell, has been described as the most famous in literature.

Jan Morris (1926–): One of the most accomplished travel writers of the twentieth century, she began life as a man but underwent gender reassignment. She worked on *The Times* and the *Guardian* before turning to full-time authorship. For a while, in the 1970s and '80s Morris lived in Bath, at No. 9 Marlborough Buildings.

Sir Walter Scott (1771–1832): Historical novelist, poet and playwright, he was the first English-language author to carve out an international career in his lifetime, with novels such as *Ivanhoe* and *Rob Roy*. As a child he stayed at No. 6 South Parade with an aunt who took him to bathe in the waters in an attempt to cure his lameness, caused by polio.

Mary Wollstonecraft Shelley (1797–1851): Best known for her Gothic horror novel *Frankenstein, or the Modern Prometheus,* she resided for a time at No. 5 Abbey Churchyard, along with her father and her future husband, Percy Bysshe Shelley. While there she continued working on her famous first novel, which she had begun while on holiday in Switzerland. *Frankenstein* was finally published anonymously in 1818.

William Makepeace Thackeray (1811–63): Novelist and satirist, most famous for his novel *Vanity Fair*, published in 1848. When in Bath he stayed with his aunt at No. 17 The Circus, which had once been Thomas Gainsborough's house.

William Wordsworth (1770–1850): The great Romantic poet stayed at No. 12 North Parade (though the plaque is, incorrectly, placed outside No. 9.) His visit was in 1841, two years after he became Poet Laureate. He, Coleridge and Southey were together known as the 'Lake Poets', and his famous poem 'Daffodils' was composed in 1804.

THE WIFE OF BATH

'A good WYF was ther of bisyde BATHE' (The Canterbury Tales)

One of the pilgrims in the famous *Canterbury Tales* by Geoffrey Chaucer (*c*. 1343–1400) is the Wife of Bath, a lady who, in addition to being a highly skilled weaver, has been much-married ('husbondes at chirche-dore she hadde fyve') and is well-travelled (she has been three times to Jerusalem). During the medieval period Bath gained a reputation for producing woollen cloth of high quality, equalling or even surpassing that of the famous Flemish weavers. Her home might well have been in nearby Twerton, where cloth making continued right up to the twentieth century.

The Wife (whose name, we learn, is Alison) tells the story of a knight at King Arthur's court who is sent on a quest to discover what it is that women most want. The answer, it transpires, is – power over their menfolk!

No. 12 Pierrepont Street was formerly a restaurant called 'The Wife of Bath' (currently occupied by the 'Yak Yeti Yak' restaurant). There is, however, a well-regarded restaurant in Wye, Kent, called 'The Wife of Bath'.

The Bath Soft Cheese Company is located in the nearby village of Kelston, and produces (among others) a semi-hard, nutty cheese called 'Wyfe of Bath', which can be bought in the Guildhall Market.

Peter Lovesey's crime novel *The Stone Wife* (Sphere, 2014), in his 'Peter Diamond' series, revolves around a stone carving of Chaucer's Wife of Bath.

In BBC television's modern adaptation of the *Canterbury Tales*, broadcast in 2003, the 'Wife of Bath' was played by Julie Walters.

JANE AUSTEN'S BATH

Some quotes about the city from her books and letters:

'Oh! Who can ever be tired of Bath?' (*Northanger Abbey*)

'Bath is a charming place, Sir; there are so many good shops here.' (*Northanger Abbey*)

'The first view of Bath in fine weather does not answer my expectations.' (Letter, 1801)

'I might try disordering my stomach with Bath buns.' (Letter, 1801)

'I really believe I shall always be talking of Bath.' (*Northanger Abbey*)

'Bath [was] preferred ... he might there be important at comparatively little expense.' (*Persuasion*)

'Why does he not try Bath? Indeed he should. Let me recommend Bath to you.' (*Emma*)

'Do you know, I get so immoderately sick of Bath?' (*Northanger Abbey*)

'The worst of Bath was the number of its plain women.' (*Persuasion*)

'Everybody acquainted with Bath may remember the difficulties of crossing Cheap Street.' (*Northanger Abbey*)

'Are you altogether pleased with Bath?' 'Yes – I like it very well.' (*Northanger Abbey*)

THE JANE AUSTEN CENTRE

Although she actually stayed at No. 25, No. 40 Gay Street has become the Jane Austen Centre in Bath. Opened in 1999, it focuses on the career of one of the city's most famous residents, her novels and how they reflect the life of the Georgian city. The centre has 'character' guides in costume, a Regency Tearoom upstairs, a Gift Shop and a waxwork of the lady herself. Guided walks around the city are also offered every weekend and special events are organised during the ten-day Jane Austen Festival each September.

As no reliable portrait of Jane Austen exists (other than a sketch by her sister, Cassandra), it was decided to commission one. Melissa Dring, a forensic artist who formerly worked with the FBI in America, was given the task of using contemporary descriptions of Jane's features and character to produce a portrait of the writer, which now hangs in the centre and was used as the basis for the waxwork.

DEAR DIARY

Some famous diarists and what they had to say about Bath in their diaries and journals:

'Much company came – many fine ladies – and the manner pretty enough, only methinks it cannot be clean to go so many bodies together into the same water.' (Samuel Pepys, June 1668)

'Went to Bath. Bought six pairs of kid gloves at Hamper's at 1s. 6d. a pair.' (Revd Francis Kilvert, September 1878)

'I shall go as often as I can to the Pump-Room, that I may drink the Water as hot from the Pump as possible, for Mr Haviland tells me, the nearer it is drunk to the Spring, the more efficacious it is.' (Revd John Penrose, April 1766)

'We all got safe to Bath (thank God) this morning about 10 o'clock, to the Castle-inn, where we made a second breakfast, and there also dined, supped and slept.' (Parson James Woodforde, June 1786)

'The farce [at the former Theatre Royal, Old Orchard Street] was 'Babes in the Wood', founded on an old ballad; but it is not exactly the same, for the poor children are preserved at last, which I was glad of, and the uncle killed. We returned late to our lodgings, had some negus [a drink made from wine, sugar, hot water, lemon juice and nutmeg], and to bed.' (Revd John Skinner, April 1803)

'The King's Bath is esteemed the fairest in Europe. The towne is intirely built of stone, but the streetes uneven, narrow and unpleasant. Here we trifled and bathed, and intervisited with the company who frequent the place for health, &c.' (John Evelyn, 1654)

'Ye Town and all its accomodations is adapted to ye batheing and drinking of the Waters and to nothing else, the Streetes are well pitched and Cleane kept and there are Chaires as in London to Carry ye better sort of people in visits, or if sick or infirme.' (Celia Fiennes, *c.* 1685)

'On the 26th April I went to Bath, and on my arrival at the Pelican Inn, found lying for me an obliging invitation from Mr. and Mrs. Thrale, by whom I was agreeably entertained almost constantly during my stay. They were gone to the Rooms; but there was a kind note from Dr Johnson, that he should sit at home all the evening.' (James Boswell, April 1776)

6

THE NATURAL WORLD

THE WATERS OF BATH

The thermal spring waters emerge at three locations in the city: The King's Bath, the Cross Bath and the Hot Bath. These lie on natural faults in the earth's crust through which the water emerges.

The spring water originated as rain, which fell on the nearby Mendip Hills at least 10,000 years ago. After permeating through the limestone rock it eventually emerges through the three 'faults' in Bath.

The combined output of the three springs is well over 200,000 gallons (1 million litres) per day. The largest of the springs is located in the King's Bath and the water rises here at the rate of 3 gallons (13 litres) per second. This is enough to fill a normal-sized domestic bath in about eight seconds!

The water is hot because it rises from a depth of around 2 miles (3km). It rises to the surface at a constant temperature of at least 113°F (45°C), making these the only true hot springs in Britain. The Bristol Hotwells, by comparison, were only about 76°F (24.5°C).

The spring water contains over forty different minerals and trace elements, including iron, calcium, lead, sulphur and magnesium. It is also very slightly radioactive.

In Georgian times, physicians would generally advise their patients to drink two or three pints of the spring water daily, but

as much as a gallon (4.5 litres) could sometimes be prescribed! This water was, and still is, served by the glass in the Pump Room. It may also be tasted at the end of the tour in the Roman Baths Museum.

The King's Bath is said to have been named after Henry I (reigned 1100–35), and the Queen's Bath after Anne of Denmark (1574–1619), wife of James I.

The modern Thermae Bath Spa, a joint Anglo/Dutch project, was opened in 2006 at a final cost of around £45 million.

In 1978 all public bathing facilities were closed when it was discovered that the waters had been contaminated by infectious organisms in the earth's upper strata, resulting in the death of a young girl. The problem was eventually solved by the drilling of boreholes to bring clean water from a lower level, but the municipal pools remained closed for twenty-eight years, until the opening of the Thermae Spa.

The water that has passed through the various Baths, together with that from the overflow, eventually travels via a system of drains into the river Avon, and thence to the sea – where the whole process starts all over again!

WHAT THEY SAID ABOUT BATH'S WATERS

Visitors who have come to 'take the waters' down the centuries have had much to say about them. Here are some quotes:

'Streams of water, warmed without human agency, and from the very bowels of the earth, rise to a receptacle beautifully constructed with chambered arches. These form baths in the middle of the city, warm and wholesome, and charming to the eye. Sick persons resort hither to bathe in the healing waters.' (*The Gesta Stephani*, 1138)

'If they can't be cured by bathing and drinking here, they will never be cured anywhere.' (Dr William Oliver, in his *Practical Dissertation on Bath-Waters*, 1719)

'I thought they wos particklery unpleasant ... I thought they'd a wery strong flavour o' warm flat-irons.' (Sam Weller, in *The Posthumous Papers of the Pickwick Club* by Charles Dickens, 1837)

'Its [*sic*] very hot and tastes like ye water that boyles Eggs, has such a smell, but ye nearer ye pumpe you drink it, ye hotter and less offencive and more spirituous.' (Celia Fiennes, in *Through England on a Side Saddle, c.* 1695)

'The colour of the water is as it were a depe blewe sea water, and reeketh like a seething Pot continually.' (John Leland, in his *Itinerary*, written 1535–43)

'These Waters have a wonderful Influence on barren Ladies, who often prove with Child even in their Husbands' Absence.' (John Macky, *A Journey through England in Familiar Letters by a Gentleman Here to his Friend Abroad*, 1722)

'If anything could make a sick man get well quickly, it would be the knowledge that he must drink a glassful of them every day until he was recovered.' (Jerome K. Jerome, in *Idle Thoughts of an Idle Fellow,* 1886)

'An old duchess of eighty and a child of four were both drinking the waters while I was there … I had a glass; it is very hot and tastes very mineral.' (William Connor Sydney, in *The Early Days of the Nineteenth Century in England,* 1811)

'I'm afraid it will be very objectionable.'

'Not at all, madam. 'Tis a little warm, and has a slight taste, but that is all.'(H.M. Bateman, *Bath Past and Present,* 1931).

'Whensoever you will go to Bathe, the Baths would strengthen your sinews.' (Sir John Harington, June 1608)

BATH'S 'LOST' SPA

Most people will probably be unaware that for almost 100 years Larkhall, a village on the north-eastern outskirts of Bath, had its own spa. A mineral spring was discovered there in 1832 when a well was sunk in order to supply water for a proposed brewery. Two years later the location was developed as a health-giving facility (the plans for the brewery were abandoned). The spa, known as the 'Larkhall' or 'Bladud' Spa, was located on land near the junction of Brooklyn and St Saviour's Roads. In 1930 the waters dried up and the building subsequently became a chapel. In 2009 Bath and North East Somerset Council erected a new road sign at Spa Lane, commemorating this important period in the village's history

BATH STONE

Since Roman times, stone has been quarried and mined from the hills around the city. In the eighteenth century the mines were acquired by the entrepreneur Ralph Allen and became very profitable with the rapid development of the city. Allen was responsible for the building of a gravity-operated railway, which ran down the hill, transporting the blocks of stone to the wharf below. By this means, Allen was enabled to reduce the cost of his stone by 25 per cent, from 10*s* to 7*s* 6*d* per ton. Extraction of Bath stone still takes place in the Corsham (Wiltshire) area, but on a much smaller scale.

SOME FACTS ABOUT BATH STONE

Bath stone is an oolitic limestone, a sedimentary rock, which was laid down in the Jurassic period (approximately 130–200 million years ago). At that time the region lay beneath warm, shallow seas in which marine sediments were deposited on the seabed. Later upheavals raised the land above sea level.

Bath stone forms part of a belt of limestone which runs diagonally from the Lyme Regis area of Dorset, through Somerset, Gloucestershire, Oxfordshire, Lincolnshire and Derbyshire before terminating in Yorkshire in the area of Whitby. Depending on the locality and variation it may be known as Portland stone, Bath stone, Cotswold stone or by various other names.

Bath stone is a 'freestone', which means that it can be cut or sawn in any direction, unlike rocks such as slate, which form layers.

The mines at Bathampton Down and Combe Down are now closed and the ones near the surface have mostly been filled with foamed concrete in order to stabilise the land. This took five years and used approximately 1½ million tons (600,000m^3) of concrete, making it the largest project of its kind in the world.

After mining operations ceased, the abandoned mines were used for a variety of purposes, including a mushroom farm and air-raid shelters during the Second World War.

As well as its extensive use in Bath, the stone was used in other cities such as London, Bristol, Reading and Truro. In London it was used on Lancaster House, Apsley House and several Victorian churches, as well as the garden frontage of Buckingham Palace.

When quarried, the stone has a light, creamy colour. Exposure to the air causes it to weather to a pale honey colour. This helps to give Bath its distinctive appearance.

Nearly ½ million tons (200,000m^3) of Bath stone were extracted to create Brunel's 2-mile (3km) long Box Tunnel in Wiltshire, opened in June 1841. The stone was used extensively in the south of England, with some being taken to Oxford for use in the colleges.

Bath stone is very susceptible to discoloration from soot and other airborne pollutants. This was a particular problem in the days before central heating and smokeless fuels became common. The cleaning of Bath stone, when it becomes necessary, must be carried out by trained professionals using accepted methods, which include water spraying, steam cleaning and, in special cases, laser cleaning or ultrasonics.

Despite being quarried fairly locally, the stone used for the facing of the SouthGate shopping development underwent a journey of 2,500 miles (4,000km) before being put in place. After being transported by lorry to Italy for cutting, it then went to Lincolnshire, where it was mounted on concrete panels before returning to Bath. This costly process attracted much criticism locally and was described as 'totally bizarre'.

PARKS AND OPEN SPACES

Bath is fortunate in having some fine parks and gardens. Here are some of them (unless otherwise stated, the parks have no admission charge):

Royal Victoria Park: This is an area of some 57 acres (23 hectares), which was officially opened in 1830 by the 11-year-old Princess Victoria. It was the first public park in England to bear her name. Privately run until 1921, it was then taken over by Bath Corporation. Its attractions include a golf course, boating pond, tennis courts, bowling green, a skateboard ramp and a children's play area. There is also a 9-acre (3.6-hectare) Botanical Garden, opened in 1887, containing one of the largest collections of limestone-loving plants in the West Country. In July 2014 the first open-air wedding ceremony to be held in the park took place.

Henrietta Park: This is named after the daughter of Sir William Pulteney, the landowner who gave his name to nearby Great Pulteney Street. It covers 7 acres (2.8 hectares), and was opened in 1897 to celebrate the Diamond Jubilee of Queen Victoria. It contains fine trees, shrubberies and flowerbeds, as well as the King George V Memorial Garden, or Garden of Remembrance as it is also known. This has a pool and fountain and is also a garden for the blind, with plants specially chosen for their scent and labels written in Braille.

Hedgemead Park: Built on a slope alongside the A4 London road, this 5-acre (2-hectare) park came about as the result of a landslide in the 1870s, which destroyed many of the houses that had been built below Camden Crescent. The area was restructured as a public park and opened in 1889. It has steps and steep paths, making access difficult for some. There is also a good example of a Victorian bandstand.

Alice Park: On the eastern edge of the city, this 8-acre (3.4-hectare) park was opened in 1937. It is named after the wife of Bath philanthropist Herbert Montgomery MacVicar of Batheaston, who gave it in trust for public use. It has tennis courts, a rose garden, a children's playground and (in summer) a café.

Parade Gardens: Stretching from Grand Parade down to the river Avon, these gardens were originally known as Harrison's Walks. They were named after Thomas Harrison, the proprietor of the eighteenth-century Assembly Rooms that once stood on the Parade. The gardens contain a bandstand (with regular concerts during the summer months), toilets and a refreshment kiosk, and the floral bedding displays are reckoned to be some of the best in Britain. There is a small admission charge for non-residents of Bath.

Sydney Gardens: Laid out in the 1790s, these are the last remaining Georgian pleasure gardens (or 'Vauxhall') in the country. The gardens are named after Viscount Sydney, the then Home Secretary. They cover about 10 acres (4 hectares) and contain trees, shrubberies, lawns and flowerbeds, as well as tennis courts and a children's play area. There is also a Temple of Minerva, originally built for the Festival of Empire in 1911. In the nineteenth century the Kennet and Avon Canal and the Great Western Railway were both routed through the gardens, using cuttings and tunnels, and there are some fine wrought-iron footbridges. The classical Sydney Hotel, now the Holburne Museum, was completed in 1799, and today houses collections of fine and decorative arts.

Prior Park Landscape Garden: Located on a hillside overlooking the city, Prior Park was once the home of the Bath entrepreneur Ralph Allen (1693–1764), owner of the stone mines. He built Prior Park mansion (now a top independent Catholic school) and laid out the gardens, with advice from Alexander Pope and 'Capability' Brown. Highlights of the gardens include the Palladian bridge, one of only four of its kind in the world, and some stunning views of Bath. The gardens are now in the care of the National Trust, so they are free to members, but there is an admission charge for non-members. It is open every day, but from November to January inclusive only at weekends. Note: there is no parking for cars.

The Georgian Garden: This is situated at the rear of No. 4 The Circus and can be accessed from the Gravel Walk. Excavations carried out in 1985–86 revealed the layout of the original garden, which was then recreated in the eighteenth-century style, using only plants that were available at the time. This was the first project of its kind in Britain. The garden is open throughout the year.

WILDLIFE IN BATH

The fish most commonly found in the river Avon around Bath are the roach, bream and gudgeon. Fish often tend to congregate around the outlet where the warm thermal water from the baths discharges into the river.

An increase in the number of otters seen in the Avon around Bath has been attributed to the improvement in water quality brought about by better sewage treatment.

In 1999, during the construction of the Bath Spa project, building work had to be temporarily halted when a mallard duck laid a clutch of six eggs at the Cross Bath. The duck, named Beatrice, together with her mate, Arthur, had been regular visitors to the spot for several years. Attempts were made to prevent their nesting by placing netting across the top of the bath, but it was repeatedly cut by duck-lovers. The nest and eggs were eventually removed under licence by Slimbridge Wildfowl Trust and the chicks hatched in an incubator.

In 2005, after evidence of peregrine activity in the area, a nesting platform was installed on the spire of St John's church in

South Parade by the Hawk and Owl Trust. The following year a pair of peregrine bred successfully and they have hatched their young here every season since. A webcam has been installed so that the public can view the nest. The birds are popular with residents and visitors, but not with the local pigeon population!

Like many built-up environments, Bath has some problems with urban foxes, which are attracted by the waste from the many food outlets in the city. Gulls are also a nuisance for the same reason, with visitors being encouraged not to feed them.

The city is home to many species of tree, a great variety of which can be found in Royal Victoria Park and the Botanical Gardens. Specimens include copper beech, leylandii, cedar, oak, maple, horse chestnut, ash, mulberry, redwood, lime, plane and the second largest Zelkova in England. Fine examples of the London plane can also be seen in Abbey Green and the group of five in The Circus known as the 'Five Sisters'. These latter, planted in the early 1800s, have often been criticised for obscuring the view of the surrounding architecture, or, as one wit expressed it: 'You can't see the Wood for the trees'.

GLOOM AND DOOM

Towards the end of the eighteenth century a farmer's daughter from Devonshire, Joanna Southcott by name, proclaimed herself as the 'Chosen One' who would produce a child who would save the world. She also made a number of prophecies, which, according to one of her disciples, included the prediction that Bath would be destroyed by an earthquake on Good Friday, 1809. With the threat from Napoleon uppermost in people's minds, there was already a heightened sense of anxiety. Because of the presence of the thermal springs, some 'experts' believed that Bath stood in the crater of an extinct volcano and panic began to spread through the city. To the dismay of local shopkeepers and lodging-house owners, people began leaving the city in large numbers. When the appointed day passed without incident, people gradually returned with, one imagines, some red faces among them!

Joanna died in 1814, but her cult still had a few followers as recently as the beginning of the twentieth century.

Geoffrey of Monmouth, in his *History of the Kings of Britain*, records what he calls the Prophecies of Merlin. King Arthur's favourite magician was apparently given to foretelling dire events that would befall the country. Among them was one concerning Bath, in which he prophesied that: 'The baths of Badon [i.e., the hot springs of Bath] shall grow cold, and their salubrious waters engender death!' He also warned that the Thames would turn to blood and the seas rise to engulf the land. Thankfully, none of these cheerful predictions has yet come to pass.

7

BELLIGERENT BATH

DUELLING

Duelling was not uncommon in Bath in the early eighteenth century, often resulting from a quarrel over gambling or a real or imagined insult. Richard 'Beau' Nash assumed the post of Bath's Master of the Ceremonies after his predecessor, Captain Webster, had been killed in a duel after an altercation over a game of cards. Nash banned the wearing of swords within the city limits in an attempt to discourage the practice of duelling. If he heard of an impending duel he would arrange to have both parties arrested.

The dell in Royal Victoria Park to the south of The Circus is still known locally as 'the Duelling Ground'. When this upper part of Bath was still unbuilt, this spot, which lay outside the city limits, was used for the settling of affairs of honour. This practice ceased when the area became residential.

During the early years of Beau Nash's reign, two 'gamesters' named Clarke and Taylor fought a duel with swords by torchlight in the Grove (Orange Grove). Oliver Goldsmith described this encounter in his *Life of Beau Nash* (1762). Clarke was the winner, running Taylor through the body, but Taylor survived for another seven years, 'when his wound, breaking out afresh, caused his death'. Clarke died in London eighteen years later in, we are told, 'poverty and contrition'. This incident gave Nash the perfect excuse for banning the wearing of swords within the city limits.

Cheating at the card table could have unfortunate consequences. During one card game a man named Newman had his hand pinned to the table with a fork by his opponent. 'Sir', said the man responsible, 'if you have not a card hidden under that hand, I apologise'. Newman later committed suicide at Bath in 1789.

Frenchman Jean Baptiste, Vicomte du Barré, died as the result of a duel in November 1778 with his friend Captain Rice (see p.136). He is buried in the churchyard of St Nicholas, Bathampton. This confrontation is often regarded as the last legal duel to be fought in Britain.

In Richard Brinsley Sheridan's play *The Rivals*, the proposed duel between Bob Acres and 'Ensign Beverley' (actually Captain Jack Absolute) is to take place in Kingsmead Fields, to the south of the city. The duel is cancelled when the combatants recognise each other.

Sheridan himself fought two duels with a certain Captain Mathews. The first was fought in an upstairs room of the Castle Tavern, Henrietta Street, and was won by Sheridan when his opponent surrendered. The second took place on Kingsdown and ended when both men were wounded. Sheridan's wounds were serious, but he eventually recovered.

In the late eighteenth and early nineteenth centuries, Lansdown, north of the city, was the venue for an annual fair, which included wrestling, cudgel matches and bare-knuckle boxing. These were often watched by members of the aristocracy and huge sums were wagered on the results. One of the most famous boxers was local man John Gully, who went on to become Champion of England and, later, a racehorse owner and Member of Parliament for Pontefract, Yorkshire.

BATTLES IN AND AROUND BATH

The Battle of Badon (*c.* late fifth century): Famous for the supposed involvement of King Arthur, this was fought between a force of Britons and Anglo-Saxons in the late fifth or early sixth century. Sometimes known as Mount Badon, it has been suggested that the 'mount' might refer to Bathampton Down. Due to the scarcity of sources there is no definite information as to the exact date of the battle, its location or details of the fighting. Other locations in England also lay claim to be the battle site.

The Battle of Dyrham (AD 577): Dyrham (or 'Deorham', as the Anglo-Saxon Chronicle calls it) lies to the north of Bath, and it was here that the battle was fought between the West Saxons and the Britons. The Saxons were led by the two chieftains, Ceawlin and his son Cuthwine, and according to the Chronicle, they defeated three kings and captured three cities: Gloucester, Cirencester and Bath. Bath then remained a Saxon town until after the Norman Conquest of 1066.

The 'Battle of the Bells' (1408): Not strictly a battle, this was a heated quarrel which broke out between the prior and the mayor. The prior claimed the right for his bell in the church of St Mary de Stalls to be the first and last to be rung each day. The independent-minded mayor opposed this and arranged for other church bells to be rung outside of the 'permitted hours'. The argument raged for years and was only finally settled in 1423 by the Bishop of Bath and Wells, who came up with a compromise that satisfied both parties: time was to be taken from the prior's clock, but the mayor's clock was permitted to be rung at certain times during the night.

The Battle of Lansdown (1643): This was fought on Lansdown Hill, to the north of Bath during the English Civil War. The Parliamentarians, under Sir William Waller, took up a position on Lansdown Hill and waited for an attack by the Royalists, commanded by Sir Ralph Hopton. The Cornish contingent of the Royalists was led by Sir Bevil Grenville. After several unsuccessful attempts to take Waller's position, during which Grenville was killed, darkness fell and the King's men retreated to wait for dawn. They could see the flickering lights of the enemy camp on the top of the hill. When dawn came and they attacked again, they found that Waller and his troops had retired to Bath and the lights they had seen were simply lengths of match which had been left hanging on the walls. Shortly after, an ammunition wagon exploded, severely wounding Hopton, and the despondent Royalist army moved away.

Today, the site of the battlefield is marked by a stone monument to Sir Bevil Grenville, erected in 1720 by his grandson, Lord Lansdown. It carries an inscription in which Sir Bevil's ancestor Sir Richard Grenville (1542–91), the great Elizabethan seaman and heroic captain of the *Revenge*, is mentioned.

Norton St Philip (1685): This village a few miles south of Bath was the site of a battle (or, more accurately, a skirmish) during the Monmouth Rebellion. On 26 June, the Duke and his followers arrived in the village and set up their headquarters. The following day the King's troops arrived, but Monmouth had taken up a strong defensive position and was able to repel their attack, and the King's army was forced to withdraw. However, a few days later Monmouth's forces suffered a final defeat at the Battle of Sedgemoor.

MILITARY BATH

A number of noted military men had a close association with the city. Here are some of them.

Major John Andre (1750–80): He was born in London (or, according to some sources, Geneva) to Huguenot parents. Educated in Geneva, he then joined the British Army, where his fluency in languages and his other abilities made him ideal for intelligence work. In 1780 he was tasked with negotiating with the American general Benedict Arnold, who had defected to the British side and had agreed to sell the plans of West Point Fort to the British. After securing the plans, Andre was captured, tried as a spy, and hanged, despite his request to die by a bullet. In 1829 his remains were returned to England and reinterred in Westminster Abbey. George Washington described him as 'more unfortunate than criminal' and as 'an accomplished man and gallant officer'. When in Bath he stayed with his parents at their home at No. 22 The Circus.

Major General Robert Clive, 1st Baron Clive (1725–74): 'Clive of India', as he became known, was born in Shropshire and at 19 he joined the East India Company as a clerk. In 1747 he gained a commission in the army and within ten years had risen to the rank of lieutenant-colonel, distinguishing himself at the Battle of Plassey (1757) and in several other campaigns. He retired from the army in 1760 and returned to England, where he received his baronetcy in 1762 and became MP for Shrewsbury. He lived in Bath for a time before moving to London, where he committed suicide at his Berkeley Square house.

General Sir Charles James Napier (1782–1853): Napier became the British Army's Commander-in-Chief in India. Born in Whitehall, London, he joined the army in 1794 and served with distinction under Wellington in the Peninsular War. He lived for a while in Henrietta Street, Bath, before being posted to India, where, in 1843, he conquered the province of Sindh when he was 61 years of age. He returned to England and died near Portsmouth, aged 71. His brother, Sir William Napier, another noted soldier, also retired to a house in Bath near Green Park.

Henry John 'Harry' Patch (1898–2009): Harry Patch was born in Combe Down, Bath, the son of a stonemason. He left school at 15 and became an apprentice plumber. Conscripted into the army in 1916, he was wounded at Passchendaele the following year and returned to England. After the war he ran a plumbing company in Somerset until his retirement at 65. In 2007 his autobiography, *The Last Fighting Tommy*, was published. He died in 2009 at the age of 111 and his funeral was held in Wells Cathedral. He is buried at St Michael's church, Monkton Combe. There is a plaque to his memory by the gates at the eastern end of Royal Avenue in Bath.

Field Marshal Frederick Sleigh Roberts, 1st Earl Roberts (1832–1914): Born in India, the son of a general, he went to the Royal Military College at Sandhurst before joining the army of the East India Company. He subsequently fought in the Indian Rebellion (where he won the Victoria Cross at the age of 26), in Abyssinia and Afghanistan, and in the Second Boer War. He then returned to India, where he achieved the rank of general and received a baronetcy. In 1895 he was given command of British forces in Ireland and was promoted to field marshal. After his retirement in 1900 he was given an earldom and was a frequent visitor to Bath, staying with his sister. 'Bobs', as he was affectionately known, died in France while visiting the Western Front and rests in St Paul's Cathedral, London.

Field Marshal George Wade (1673–1748): Born in Tangiers, North Africa, where his father was a serving soldier, he joined the army when the family returned to their Irish home. He served under Marlborough in Flanders and was promoted to general at the age of 35. He was sent to Bath in 1715 to participate in the suppression of a Jacobite Rising, and unearthed a large cache of weapons. In 1722 he was elected MP for Bath, a seat he held for twenty-five years, and had a house in Abbey Churchyard (now a shop). He campaigned in Scotland, where he built many roads and bridges. He became a field marshal in 1743 and died in London at the age of 75. He is buried in Westminster Abbey.

Major-General James Wolfe (1727–59): Wolfe was born in Kent, but the family moved to London in about 1738. His ambition was to join the army (his father was an officer) and he joined the Marines at the age of 13. He served in Europe before his regiment was recalled to Britain to deal with the Jacobite Rising. He then fought in the Seven Years' War against France. His parents had taken a house in Trim Street, Bath, where he often visited them. It was here, in 1758, that he received the news that he had been given command of the Quebec expedition. The opposing forces met on the Plains of Abraham and, although Quebec was captured, Wolfe was mortally wounded. At the time of his death he was 32, and he is buried at St Alfege's church, Greenwich. There is a monument to him in Westminster Abbey.

NAUTICAL BATH

Not to be outdone by the military, Bath has had its share of famous naval heroes:

Vice Admiral Horatio Nelson, 1st Viscount Nelson (1758–1805): Born in Norfolk, Nelson joined the Royal Navy at 12 years of age, rising to the rank of captain within ten years. During his distinguished career he lost the sight of his right eye (1794) and most of his right arm (1797). He stayed in Bath on many occasions, usually to recuperate after long voyages, occupying lodgings in Pierrepont Street. On his visit in 1780 he had to be carried to the baths, being too ill to walk. In 1801 he received a viscountcy and was promoted to vice admiral. At the Battle of Trafalgar he was mortally wounded and his body was returned to England in a barrel of brandy. He was interred at St Paul's Cathedral in a sarcophagus originally intended for Cardinal Wolsey.

Rear Admiral Sir Edward Berry (1768–1831): A great friend of Nelson, and one of his most trusted captains, Nelson referred to Berry as his 'right hand' (having lost his own). Berry was Nelson's flag captain at the Battle of the Nile (1798) and commanded the *Agamemnon* at Trafalgar. On his retirement he lived in Gay Street until his death.

Admiral Richard Howe, 1st Earl Howe (1726–99): The highlight of Howe's distinguished naval career was his victory at the Battle of Ushant in 1794 in what became known as the 'Glorious First of June'. This led to his promotion to Admiral of the Fleet two years later. Between 1780 and his death he visited Bath regularly, sometimes staying for months at a time at his house in Great Pulteney Street.

Admiral Sir William Hargood (1762–1839): Hargood joined the Royal Navy as a midshipman, aged 13, and served with distinction in the American War of Independence and the Napoleonic Wars. At Trafalgar he commanded the *Belleisle,* a ship of the line which had been captured from the French some years before. After peace was declared in 1815 he was knighted and retired to the Royal Crescent in Bath, where he died, aged 77. He is buried in Bath Abbey.

Admiral Alexander Hood (1727–1814): Hood was second in command to Lord Howe at the 'Glorious First of June' engagement during the French Revolutionary War. He was created Viscount Bridport in 1801. After a long and distinguished career he retired to Bath, living in Great Pulteney Street until his death.

With a much shorter history than either the army or the navy, the air force has few historic connections with Bath and has produced only one notable pilot that I have been able to find.

Wing Commander John Robert Baldwin (?–1952) was born in Bath. He became an officer in the RAF Volunteer Reserve and a top scoring fighter ace during the Second World War. Between 1943 and 1947 he was awarded the DFC and Bar and the DSO and Bar. During the Korean War he was attached to the US Air Force and was posted missing, presumed killed, in 1952.

BLITZ ON BATH

In April 1942 Bath suffered a series of three air raids as part of the so-called 'Baedeker Blitz' – reprisals for the RAF raids that had devastated the German city of Lübeck the previous month. The Luftwaffe's selected targets in this case were of cultural and historical, rather than military, significance, and were identified using the 'Baedeker' travel guide for Britain. Any building marked with three stars in the guide was to be regarded as a potential target. Over 400 people were killed and around 19,000 buildings damaged or destroyed in the city. Little remains today to show the effects of the raids, but if you know where to look, there is still some evidence.

St Andrew's church, which stood behind the Royal Crescent, was gutted by incendiary bombs and finally demolished in 1957 – only a grassy plot remains.

The Genesis Trust building on the corner of James Street West and Kingsmead North is one of the last remaining examples of bomb damage in Bath. The walls of this Grade II listed building bear the scars of shrapnel, while the upper storey was destroyed by incendiary bombs.

The Assembly Rooms in Bennett Street were severely damaged by incendiary bombs. They were restored and reopened in 1963, but evidence of the fire can still be seen in the form of pink scorch marks on the walls of the Tea Room.

A number of manufacturing companies in Bath were engaged in the production of items for military use. These included gun mountings, torpedo parts and aircraft propellers.

In 1939 the Admiralty moved its entire warship design operation to Bath from London, taking over the Empire Hotel, Orange Grove. They finally moved out in 1989, on the expiration of the fifty-year lease.

In April 2008 Willi Schludecker, an 88-year-old former Luftwaffe bomber pilot, visited Bath and made a public apology to the people of the city for his part in the 1942 raids.

COME TO BATH – AND BE INSULTED!

Residents of (and visitors to) Bath could be very outspoken at times. Here are a few examples of plain speaking that have gone on record:

Lord Chesterfield, a regular visitor to Bath for thirty years, wrote a series of letters to his son, giving him advice on manners and deportment. Dr Samuel Johnson, another regular, was not impressed by these letters, declaring that they 'taught the morals of a whore and the manners of a dancing master'.

Philip Thicknesse, irascible one-time resident of the Royal Crescent, appealed to his mother-in-law for help when he and his family were stricken with diphtheria. The lady refused to help him. His wife and two of his children died, and the bitter Thicknesse wrote the following to his late wife's mother: 'Madam, your daughter is dead, your grandchildren are dead, and I apprehend I am dying; but if I ever recover, the greatest consolation I can have is that now, I have no more to do with you'.

If any gentleman were so ill-advised as to appear at an Assembly Ball wearing riding boots, Beau Nash would pointedly ask him, in front of the company, if he had forgotten his horse! On one notable occasion, when the Duchess of Queensberry appeared wearing a fashionable lace apron worth £200, Nash showed his disapproval by forcibly removing it and throwing it to a servant.

Despite their being on good terms, Samuel Johnson found the husband of his long-time friend Mrs Hester Thrale somewhat dull, and declared that 'his conversation does not show the minute hand, but he strikes the hour very correctly'.

Beau Nash was known to have a sharp tongue on occasion. While suffering from an illness he was visited by the well-known Bath physician Dr George Cheyney, who prescribed some medicine. Meeting the Master of Ceremonies in the street a few days later, the good doctor observed that he was pleased to see that Nash had followed his prescription. Nash replied that, had he done so, he would have broken his neck, as he had thrown it from an upstairs window!

There were times, however, when the Beau met his match. On two occasions he got the worst of an encounter with the famous evangelist John Wesley. The first was when he tried to disrupt one of Wesley's open-air meetings, only to retire in defeat when both the preacher and his supporters bested him with words.

On another occasion, a sharp exchange between Nash and Wesley apparently took place in Brock Street. Nash and some of his friends encountered Wesley coming in the opposite direction. The pavement was not wide enough to allow them to pass, and someone would have to give way. Nash is reputed to have said that he 'did not step aside for fools and knaves', to which Wesley replied that *he* always did – and moved aside!

In 1734 Prince William of Orange visited the city twice, to take the waters. A very short man with a hunched back, he was described by Lord Hervey as looking from the front as if he had no neck or legs, and from the back as if he had no head! His breath, according to Hervey, was 'more offensive than it is possible for those who have not been offended by it to imagine'.

8

SPIRES, SAINTS
AND SPOOKS

PLACES OF WORSHIP

Some facts about Bath Abbey:

There has been a church on this site for well over 1,000 years; first a Saxon church, then a Norman monastery, and finally the abbey we see today.

Work on the present abbey was begun in 1499 under the Bishop of Bath and Wells, Oliver King. His name can be seen on two buttresses on the abbey's West Front, in the form of a 'rebus', or word picture. It depicts a bishop's mitre (Bishop) surmounting an olive tree (Oliver) encircled with a crown (King).

The tower is oblong in section rather than square, because it was built on the foundations of a bay of the nave of the Norman church which previously stood on the site. The present abbey occupies only the space taken up by the old Norman nave.

The bases of the massive columns of the Norman abbey can still be seen through a grating in the floor to the left of the Sanctuary.

The abbey has more plaques and monuments (over 640) on its interior walls than any other church in the country, with the exception of Westminster Abbey.

The beautiful fan vaulting in the nave is actually Victorian, having been constructed in the 1860s to match the Tudor vaulting in the choir. Up until then, the nave had a flat, plaster roof.

The angels and ladders on the west front recall those which Bishop King claimed to have seen in a dream in which he was urged to rebuild the ruined Norman church.

The statues on either side of the West Door are those of Sts Peter and Paul, to whom the abbey is dedicated. Peter's head (on the left) was destroyed, probably by the actions of Parliamentary soldiers during the English Civil War, and a new head was carved from the stump of his neck.

The great carved West Doors were a gift from Sir Henry Montagu, Lord Chief Justice to King James I. His brother James Montagu was Bishop of Bath and Wells at the time.

The abbey's exceptionally light interior, due to its fifty-two windows, has led to its nickname of 'The Lantern of the West'.

It is believed that a *tholos*, or small, circular Roman temple, once stood on the site of what is now the west end of the abbey.

The abbey contains 891 Ledger Stones; flat stones placed over graves beneath the floor of a church. They are usually inscribed with the name and dates of the person buried there. In Bath Abbey they mostly date from the late 1600s to the late 1700s.

In addition to the abbey, there were many other religious buildings in the city, catering for a variety of creeds and beliefs.

The Roman Catholic Church of St John the Evangelist: With its 222ft (68m) spire, this stands at the end of South Parade. It was built in 1861–63 to the design of Charles Francis Hansom (brother of Joseph, the inventor of the Hansom cab). The church was commissioned by the Benedictines of Downside Abbey and is modelled on the late thirteenth- to early fourteenth-century Decorated style. The church was bombed in 1942 and the south aisle was destroyed and subsequently rebuilt. The first evening service to be held here was conducted by Cardinal Newman.

The Countess of Huntingdon's Chapel in the Vineyards: Built in 1765 in the Gothic Revival style, it was constructed for Selina Hastings, Countess of Huntingdon (1707–91), a Methodist who eventually disagreed with John Wesley on matters of doctrine and broke away to form her own 'connexion'. Through her aristocratic background and forceful personality, she kept tight control over her sect, training and appointing her own ministers, despite opposition from the Church of England. The connexion still has around twenty active churches in England, but the Bath chapel is now home to the Museum of Bath Architecture. Huntingdon County, Pennsylvania and Huntingdon College in Montgomery, Alabama, are both named after the countess.

The Octagon Chapel, Milsom Street: The chapel was designed by Timothy Lightoler and opened in 1767. Its octagonal shape made it popular with preachers, including John Wesley, because the congregation could sit closer to the pulpit than in a traditional rectangular chapel. It was built by subscription and pews would be rented for private use. As such, it did not need to be consecrated. The chapel achieved very fashionable status, with notables such as Jane Austen attending services. Its resident organist was the celebrated musician and astronomer William Herschel (discoverer of the planet Uranus).

After it fell into disuse, the chapel served a variety of purposes, and during Second World War it was used as a food store. Later it became the headquarters of the Royal Photographic Society. Today, as a Grade II* listed building, the chapel is used for exhibitions and events, and is surrounded by retail development.

St Swithin's C of E Church, Walcot: The present church dates from 1777, and stands on the site of earlier churches dating back to Saxon times. It is the only remaining eighteenth century parish church in Bath and is built in the Classical style. The architect was John Palmer (designer of Lansdown Crescent), who later extended the building when it became too small. Inside the church are many memorials to the notable people who worshipped there. The parents of Jane Austen, the Revd George Austen and Cassandra Leigh, were married here, but that was in the previous church of 1742. In the churchyard can be seen a memorial to Jane's father, who is buried in the church vault.

St Stephen's C of E Church, Lansdown: Built 1840–45 to the design of James Wilson, at a cost of £6,000, it is constructed of limestone from the former Limpley Stoke quarries and is in a Victorian Gothic style. The tower starts square and then becomes octagonal; Sir Nikolaus Pevsner called it 'crazy'. The crypt was converted into a community centre in the 1990s.

St Michael with St Paul C of E Church, Broad Street: Built in 1834–37 to a design by George Philip Manners, it replaced an earlier eighteenth-century church known as St Michael Without (i.e., outside the city walls). Today's church is in the Early English style with tall windows and a thin spire and the architect is said to have taken his inspiration from Salisbury Cathedral. It is a 'hall church', in which the side aisles are the same height as the nave. The church has a coffee shop with homemade cakes.

Manvers Street Baptist Church: Built in the Gothic Revival style, this is the work of Willson and Wilcox, and dates from 1871–72, with an extension built in 1907. Its west front, with its arches and turret, is based on designs of early French Cistercian churches. The Victorian period saw a considerable growth in church membership and in particular of Nonconformism. The church runs a café and open house centre and is home to several other welfare organisations.

St Mary the Virgin, Raby Place, Bathwick: Designed by John Pinch the Elder, it opened in 1820. It is typical of the nineteenth-century Gothic Revival, and is undoubtedly one of Bath's finest late-Georgian Anglican churches. The tower is over 100ft (30.5m) high and has had favourable comparison with that of Bath Abbey.

The Friends' Meeting House, York Street: Built in 1817–19 as a Masonic Hall, the architect was William Wilkins and the style is Classical. The Freemasons moved to other premises in 1841 and the building was used by others, including Baptists, for a while, before becoming the Meeting House of the Religious Society of Friends, or 'Quakers', in the mid-twentieth century.

Other Faiths

Muslims in Bath can meet at the Al Muzaffar Mosque, located in the basement of a Georgian terraced house in Pierrepont Street. The house was acquired in the 1990s and is run by the Bath Islamic Society. It is named after a Palestinian businessman, Diya Eddin Muhiyeddin Al-Muzaffar, who owned the house and subsequently sold it to the BIS for use as a mosque.

Bath currently has no synagogue, its small Jewish community mostly tending to worship in Bristol, but there was formerly a synagogue in Kingsmead Street (now James Street West), which opened in about 1800. The site is now occupied by a DHSS building. Around 1840 a second synagogue was opened in Corn Street. However, the Jewish community in Bath declined, and by 1911 both synagogues had closed.

There is no Gurdwara, or Sikh Temple, in Bath, the nearest being in Bristol. The same applies to Hindu Temples.

CHURCH CURIOSITIES

Because it had to be fitted into an awkward space at the junction of Walcot and Broad Streets, St Michael's church lies on a north-south axis, unlike most Christian churches, which lie east-west so that the congregation is facing towards the Holy Land. This church is a 'hall church', that is, the aisles are the same height as the nave. This style is not common in Britain.

St Michael's has an unusual modern communion table, designed and made by Stephen Budd. The legs are made from 5,000-year-old Glastonbury bog oak and the top from burr elm. It can be seen as representing different aspects of Christianity.

The north apse of St John's Catholic church is said to house relics of St Justina of Padua, a fourth-century saint who was martyred during the persecutions of the Roman emperor Diocletian. The relics were found centuries ago in the catacombs of Rome and were given to St John's in 1871.

The wrought-iron rood screen in St John's has an image of a 'pelican in her piety', feeding her young with her own blood. This is a medieval symbol representing Christ shedding his blood for humankind.

In Bath Abbey, the Quire Screens display twelve carved angels playing a variety of musical instruments. These were designed by Paul Fletcher and carved in lime wood by Laurence Beckford. They were installed in October 2007.

SAINTS IN BATH

Many locations in Bath are named after saints. Here are just some of them:

St Andrew: Apostle and patron saint of Scotland and Russia. A community church in Combe Down is dedicated to him and also a primary school in Northampton Road. A St Andrew's church once stood in Julian Road, behind the Royal Crescent, but it was destroyed by bombs in 1942.

St James (St James the Greater): Apostle and patron saint of Spain and of pilgrims. He gives his name to various thoroughfares in the city, including St James's Parade and James Street West.

St James's church (also destroyed by wartime bombs) formerly stood in Lower Borough Walls.

St John the Baptist: Cousin of Jesus who prophesied his coming. He gives his name to the St John's Hospital, founded in 1174 by Bishop FitzJocelin and among the oldest almshouses in the country. The group of four houses next to the Theatre Royal, which include the former home of Beau Nash, were formerly known as St John's Court.

St John the Evangelist (also known as St John the Divine): Apostle and gospel writer. He gives his name to the Roman Catholic church in South Parade and also to one in nearby Lower Weston.

St Mark: Evangelist and gospel writer. He gives his name to a Church of England school, a community centre and two streets in Bath.

St Mary (or St Mary the Virgin): Mother of Jesus. She has two churches in Bath dedicated to her, one Roman Catholic and one Church of England, and also a RC primary school.

St Michael: Archangel and leader of the celestial armies. The church in Broad Street is dedicated to him, as is the chapel attached to St John's Hospital. Also, of course, he is the 'patron saint' of Marks and Spencer, who have a store on Stall Street. Bath also has a St Michael's Court and a St Michael's Place.

St Paul: Apostle to the Gentiles. He is commemorated (jointly with St Michael) in the church at the bottom of Broad Street, and with St Peter at Bath Abbey and at the Catholic church on Entry Hill.

St Peter: Apostle and keeper of the keys of heaven. He gives his name to St Peter's Terrace, East Twerton (in addition to the Bath Abbey).

St Stephen: The first Christian martyr. He is commemorated in the church dedicated to him at Lansdown, a primary school and four streets in the city.

GRAVE MATTERS

There are a number of cemeteries and burial grounds in Bath, some of which are the final resting places of prominent people.

In Roman times burials were not permitted within the town limits, bodies being interred outside the walls. This applied to Bath, and a large number of Roman tombstones and funerary monuments have been uncovered, giving us a picture of life in Aquae Sulis between the first and fourth centuries AD. One is a memorial to Successa Petronia, a little girl who lived for three years, four months and nine days, erected by her grieving parents. Another records the death of a local senator who passed away at the age of 80. Examples can be seen today in the Roman Baths Museum.

In addition to the hundreds of bodies interred beneath its floor, Bath Abbey has its own cemetery. It is located on Ralph Allen Drive, Widcombe, and was opened in 1844. There are a number of clerical and military figures buried here, including the aptly named Rear Admiral John Bythesea, a VC recipient from the Crimean War. The Roman Catholic Perrymead Cemetery is located nearby.

Locksbrook Cemetery is situated on the Upper Bristol Road at Lower Weston. Opened in 1864, its 12-acre (about 5-hectare) site contains more than 30,000 interments, but was closed for general use in 1937. It has been designated as a Nature Conservation Site by its owners, Bath and North East Somerset Council. It contains a total of 122 military graves which are in the care of the Commonwealth War Graves Commission. Three holders of the Victoria Cross, who all served in India in the nineteenth century, are buried here.

Smallcombe Cemetery is situated in a valley on the south-eastern edge of Bath. It is divided into two parts: the Anglican section and the Nonconformist section. Burials began here in

1856, and the site was closed for new burials in 1988. Among the graves here are those of composer Fred Weatherly ('Danny Boy', 'Roses of Picardy'), the parents of the poet A.E. Housman and several recipients of the Victoria Cross.

The Jewish Burial Ground is at Bradford Road on Combe Down, at the edge of the old city limits, and was opened in 1812. It is one of the few indications left of the former Hebrew congregation in Bath. The grounds contain a little Ohel (chapel or prayer house), which was later used as a caretaker's cottage. There are about fifty tombstones in the cemetery, which has Grade II listed status. It is one of only fifteen such cemeteries to have survived from the Georgian era.

Opposite the Royal National Hospital for Rheumatic Diseases in Upper Borough Walls is a short stretch of reconstructed city wall. Behind this is a low area that formerly served as the burial ground for the hospital. Founded in 1738 as the General Hospital, it later became the Mineral Water Hospital. It provided care for those sick visitors to Bath who could not afford the spa facilities. They were required to bring a letter of authorisation from their home parish plus the sum of £3. This was to cover the cost of their return fare if they were cured, or their burial if not. Those patients who died were buried in the small graveyard until it became full and was closed in 1849. In all, 238 bodies were interred here.

HAUNTED BATH

Some of the ghosts and other apparitions that reputedly haunt various locations in the city:

The Man in the Black Hat: A strange figure in eighteenth-century dress, with a tall black hat. There have been many reported sightings, usually in the neighbourhood of the Assembly Rooms in Bennett Street. He is thought by some to be possibly Admiral Arthur Phillip (1738–1814), the first Governor of New South Wales who died at No. 19.

The Grey Lady: Seen in the Theatre Royal (claimed to be Britain's most haunted theatre) and in the neighbouring Italian restaurant, formerly a house once occupied by Beau Nash. As she wafts around, she invariably leaves behind her the scent of jasmine.

A British soldier: He is dressed in a First World War uniform and has been seen in a dark corner of the Crown Inn, Bathwick Street, drinking a ghostly pint of beer.

Admiral Earl Howe (1726–99): The ghost of the famous naval commander of the American War of Independence and the French Revolutionary Wars is said to haunt No. 71 Great Pulteney Street, his former home.

'Bunty': A Victorian worker at the former Beehive Pub (now the Grappa Bar). She makes occasional appearances wearing a grey-blue gown, and is said to be 'non-threatening'.

A medieval monk: Cowled and robed, he is seen in the vicinity of the Crystal Palace Pub in Abbey Green. This was originally part of the abbey precincts, prior to the Dissolution.

'Sylvia': a former housekeeper to John Wood I who hanged herself in a fit of depression in 1731. Her ghost has been seen and heard on a number of occasions in the Francis Hotel, part of which was once Wood's house.

A ghostly carriage and four: This has occasionally been seen in the neighbourhood of the Royal Crescent and has sometimes been thought to be linked to the elopement of Elizabeth Linley and Richard Brinsley Sheridan in 1772.

Some people claim to have seen, in the vicinity of the abbey, the apparition of 'a naked Roman soldier' – which, of course, poses the question: how were they able to tell what he was?

Here is a more modern example, as related by Roy Wilcox, a former Bath police officer:

Early one Christmas morning in the 1960s, two police officers were patrolling their beat in central Bath. Making their way along Sawclose, they stopped outside the stage door of the Theatre Royal and noticed that it was slightly ajar. The theatre should have been completely empty and locked by then. The nearby streets were deserted. The policemen entered, switched on their torches and made their way along the corridor, inspecting the rooms as they went. Eventually they reached the auditorium, where they checked the seats to make sure no tramp had come in to seek a night's shelter. No sign of anyone, but as they turned to leave, one of them had a thought. He'd always wanted to 'tread the boards' since appearing in a school play, so he persuaded his colleague to join him on the stage, where they performed a soft-shoe shuffle, using their torches as spotlights and helmets as props. Finishing their routine, they took a bow. Suddenly, from out of the darkness, came the dull, rhythmic sound of a single person clapping. Shining their torches on the exact spot from which the sound was coming, they saw – nothing! The two officers exited the theatre smartly, slamming the door behind them. Colleagues, not believing their story, went to check the theatre, but there was not a soul there. Or was there?

9

CRIME AND
PUNISHMENT

Bath could be a dangerous place, even in the more salubrious areas.

In 1828 a servant named Maria Bagnall was murdered at a house in Marlborough Buildings by Richard Gilham, a fellow servant. He tried to disguise his crime as a botched robbery attempt, but was found out and convicted. He was hanged and his body given to the Royal United Hospital for dissection.

In the eighteenth century the roads into Bath were infested with highwaymen, out for rich pickings from wealthy visitors. The worst of these was a gang led by John Poulter, a notorious ruffian. On one occasion he stopped a coach carrying a Dr

Hancock and his young daughter and threatened the child's life. This resulted in a hue and cry and the offer of a large reward. Poulter was soon taken, convicted and subsequently hanged. His body was afterwards displayed on the gibbet at Claverton Down, close to the scene of his last robbery.

In August 1799 Mrs Jane Leigh Perrot, an aunt of Jane Austen, was arrested for shoplifting. It was claimed that she had stolen a card of lace from a Bath haberdasher's, a crime that warranted the penalty of transportation if convicted. At her subsequent trial in Taunton she was speedily acquitted. It became apparent that those at the shop had planted the lace in the hope of extorting money in exchange for dropping the charge.

Prostitution was rife in Victorian Bath and some areas of the lower city, such as Avon Street, were 'red light' districts. The Revd William Jay Bolton, sometime vicar of St James, Stall Street, spent the last three years of his life engaged in a one-man campaign against the trade, buying up brothels and turning them into respectable dwellings. He subsequently wrote a booklet about his struggles. He died at Bath in 1884 at the age of 67.

In the fifteenth century a pillory and stocks were erected in the market place outside the abbey and there was also a ducking stool by the river at Boatstall Quay. These were used as temporary punishments for offences such as dishonest trading or malicious gossip. Those confined in them could be pelted with rotten fruit. The location of these devices can be seen on the map produced by Joseph Gilmore in 1694.

Born near Bath in 1750, John Rann, known as 'Sixteen String Jack' from his habit of wearing coloured strings on the knees of his britches, was a highwayman who became famous for his wit and colourful exploits. He was publicly hanged at Tyburn in 1774 at the age of 24.

Some types of offender could be sent to the Bridewell, or House of Correction, which stood near the present Theatre Royal. 'Bridewells', for the incarceration of petty offenders, had been introduced during the reign of Elizabeth I and the first one had been built near St Bride's (or Bridget's) Well in London – hence the name.

Not everyone seems to have regarded Bath as a lawless place. John Wood the Elder, in his famous 1749 'Essay' on Bath, writes: 'Honesty ... has been so prevalent at Bath, that very little Use hath been made of any of her Prisons, notwithstanding the Opportunities and Temptations for Robbery have been greater here than perhaps in any publick Place of the Kingdom.'

In the early 1800s an organisation was formed in Bath known as The Society of Guardians, which existed 'for the protection of persons and property from felons, forgers, receivers of stolen goods, cheats, swindlers, highwaymen &c'. It was supported by voluntary contributions from citizens of 5 shillings per year, which would entitle them to their expenses 'in advertising, apprehending and prosecuting offenders'.

In 1836 Bath became the first city outside London to create its own police force. This came about as a result of the Municipal Corporation Act of the previous year. The first Superintendent was Captain William F. Carroll, RN (retd), who had charge of about 140 officers. Early police officers wore top hats and swallowtail coats, and were equipped with a rattle and a truncheon. Cutlasses could be issued in the event of serious trouble.

Confidence tricksters were at least as common in the eighteenth century as they are now. The following is an extract from the *Bath Chronicle* of 2 February 1764:

On Sunday Evening, a Man went to a Pastry-Cook's Shop on Cheap-street, and ordered half a dozen tarts to be carried to a House on the Borough-Walls, together with Change for a Guinea. The Maid was sent with it accordingly, but was met in the Market-Place by the Man, who desir'd her to give him the Change, telling her he was going for some Wine, and that she was to have the Guinea on her delivering the Tarts to the House. The Girl very readily gave him the Money, but to her great Surprise, when she came to the House, she found the People knew nothing of the Affair, nor had they given Orders for any Tarts ... many Attempts of the same Kind were made on different Shop-Keepers last Week.

In 1896 two killers, for whom police all over Britain had been searching, were apprehended in Bath. Henry Fowler and Albert Milsom had murdered an elderly man in London and were eventually traced to a house in Monmouth Street, where they were arrested by Chief Inspector Noble and Inspector Newport after a desperate struggle. The two men confessed to the crime and were subsequently hanged at London's Newgate.

In 1951, serial killer John Thomas Straffen abducted (and later killed) five-year-old Brenda Goddard from the garden of No. 1 Camden Crescent. She was the first of his three child victims, two of whom lived in Bath. Straffen was eventually caught and sentenced to life imprisonment. He became the longest-serving prisoner in British legal history and died in 2007.

Former multi-millionaire businessman John Palmer, who owned a Georgian mansion near Bath, was acquitted in 1987 of handling gold bullion from the Brinks-Mat robbery of 1983. It was alleged that he had melted down some of the bullion in the garden of his then home, Battlefields. However, Palmer, nicknamed 'Goldfinger', was later convicted of a huge timeshare fraud and in 2001 was sentenced to eight years' imprisonment, of which he served four. In June 2015 he was shot dead at his home in Essex.

During the year 2013–14, 4,600 crimes were recorded in the city, the vast majority being committed in the central area. Of these, almost half consisted of anti-social behaviour and a further 14 per cent of shoplifting.

Vandalism, too, is nothing new. The *Bath Chronicle* of 16 May 1799 reported: 'WHEREAS FOUR SEDAN-CHAIRS, standing in different parts of the city, were last night wilfully CUT and DEFACED by some person or persons unknown:- Whoever will discover the offender or offenders ... shall receive FIVE GUINEAS Reward ... by order of the Mayor.'

FICTIONAL BATH DETECTIVES

Some authors of popular crime novels have chosen to set their stories in Bath.

Detective Superintendent Peter Diamond is head of the Murder Squad at Bath's CID in the series of books by Peter Lovesey, beginning with *The Last Detective* (1991). Lovesey is also the creator of Sergeant Cribb, the Victorian detective.

Detective Inspector James Boswell Hodge Leonard is the eccentric protagonist in a series of novels starting with *The Bath Detective* (1995). The author is Christopher Lee (the writer and historian, not the late actor).

Sara Selkirk is the international cellist and amateur sleuth in *Funeral Music* (1998) and other novels by Morag Joss.

Jack Swann is a consulting detective to the Bow Street Runners, who gets involved with dark doings in Bath. He features in *The Regency Detective* (2013) by Bath authors David Lassman and Terence James.

Detective Inspector Zoe Benedict is the Bath police officer with a secret in the novel *Hanging Hill* (2011) by Mo Hayder.

Police Constable Sally Gentle is the principal character in the series of comedy/crime novels set in Bath and written by Sandy Osborne, who drew on her own experiences as a West Country police officer. The first, *Girl Cop*, was published in 2012.

Colin Dexter's famous creation Detective Chief Inspector Endeavour Morse pays a visit to the city in the novel *Death is now my Neighbour* (1996), the twelfth book in the popular series.

Although not actually a fictional character, the writer Jane Austen features, in the role of amateur sleuth, in a series of novels by the American author Stephanie Barron. So far at least a dozen have been written, beginning with *Jane and the Unpleasantness at Scargrave Manor* (1996). Some of these novels have Bath as a setting.

THE CURSE OF BATH

In Roman Bath it was the custom to cast votive offerings into the sacred spring, usually in the hope of achieving a desired result. Many of these offerings have been recovered and can be seen in the Roman Baths Museum. They would sometimes take the form of curses, inscribed on sheets of pewter and written backwards (so that only the gods could read them). It was hoped that the gods appealed to would exact retribution on the perpetrators, because, of course, they would know their identity, even if the victim did not. Here are a few examples.

'May he who carried off Vilbia from me become as liquid as the water. May she who so obscenely devoured her become dumb ...' Then follows a list of possible suspects. Maybe the gods could make some sense of it!

Another, from someone who has had money stolen, reads: 'To the goddess Sulis Minerva ... I give to your divinity the money I have lost, that is five denarii, and may he who has stolen it, whether slave or free, whether man or woman, is to be compelled...' (at this point the curse breaks off).

Most of the curses are connected with a theft: 'Solinus to the goddess Sulis Minerva. I give to your divinity and majesty [my] bathing tunic and cloak. Do not allow sleep or health to him who has done me wrong, whether man or woman or whether slave or free unless he reveals himself and brings those goods to your temple.'

And finally: 'Docimedis has lost two gloves, and asks that the thief responsible should lose their mind and their eyes in the goddess' temple.'

Strong stuff, but probably good psychology. If the thief knew that such a curse had been laid, it might have caused him or her a few sleepless nights! About 130 of these curses have so far been recovered.

10

THE SOCIAL SCENE

By the mid-1700s Bath had become England's most fashionable resort. The diversions and entertainments took place under the watchful eye of a Master of the Ceremonies, a post that carried the responsibility for ensuring that appropriate standards of dress and conduct were observed by visitors.

HOW TO BEHAVE WHEN IN BATH

The great Beau Nash, on his appointment as Master of the Ceremonies, drew up his own set of rules covering dress and behaviour which all visitors were expected to obey. These were posted in various locations throughout the town.

THE RULES OF BATH (By general Consent determin'd)
I. That a Visit of Ceremony at coming to Bath, and another at going away, is all that is expected or desired by Ladies of Quality and Fashion – except Impertinents.
II. That Ladies coming to the Ball appoint a Time for their Footmen coming to wait on them Home, to prevent Disturbances and Inconveniences to Themselves and Others.
III. That Gentlemen of Fashion never appearing in a Morning before the Ladies in Gowns and Caps, shew Breeding and Respect.
IV. That no person take it ill that any one goes to another's play or breakfast, and not to theirs – except captious by nature.
V. That no Gentleman give his tickets for the Balls to any but

Gentlemen – N.B. Unless he has none of his acquaintance.

VI. That Gentlemen crowding before Ladies at the Ball, shew ill-manners; and that none do so for the Future – except such as respect nobody but Themselves.

VII. That no Gentleman or Lady takes it ill that another Dances before them – except such as have no Pretence to dance at all.

VIII. That the Elder Ladies and Children be contented with a second bench at the Ball, as being past or not come to Perfection.

IX. That the Younger Ladies take notice how many Eyes observe them – N.B. This does not extend to the Have-at-Alls.

X. That all Whisperers of Lies and Scandal be taken for their Authors.

XI. That all Repeaters of such Lies and Scandal be shunn'd by all Company – except such as have been guilty of the same Crime.

Some years later, Nash must have felt that standards were starting to slip, because he made the following additions:

Whereas Politeness, Decency and Good-manners, three ancient Residents at Bath, have, of late, left the Place; whoever shall restore them, shall be rewarded with Honour and Respect.

Gentlemen coming into the Rooms in Boots, where Ladies are, shew their little Regard to them or the Company: Except they have no Shoes.

Ladies dressing and behaving like Handmaids must not be surprized if they are treated as Handmaids.

Whisperers of Lies and Scandal, knowing them to be such, are rather worse than the Inventors.

A lot for visitors to remember; but then, if you wanted your stay in Bath to be a pleasant one, it was *not* a good idea to risk offending the Beau!

MASTERS OF THE CEREMONIES

Although Beau Nash is easily the most famous of Bath's Masters of the Ceremonies, he was by no means the only person to occupy the post.

Captain Webster, the first true MC at Bath, was appointed by the Duke of Beaufort in the first years of the eighteenth century. He was killed in a duel over a game of cards in 1710, and was succeeded by Richard Nash, who for several years had been acting as his assistant.

Mr Collett (or M. Colette – he may have been French; first name unknown) had acted as assistant to Nash, and, on the death of the Beau in 1761, became his immediate successor. His personality and abilities were not, however, suited to the post, and he kept the position for only two years.

Samuel Derrick, an Irish author and failed actor, succeeded to the post in 1763. Like Nash, he was also MC at Tunbridge Wells, Kent, travelling between the two locations. He remained in post until his death in 1769. A man of small stature, his tenure was not a great success: the writer James Boswell called him a 'little blackguard'. Despite being in receipt of an income of £800 per year, at his death he was penniless and a public appeal was needed to pay for his funeral.

Captain William Wade was appointed to the post (which he held jointly with the town of Brighton) in 1769. Noted for his elegance and good looks, he was known as 'The Bath Adonis', but his fondness for the ladies led to his being involved in a marital scandal, and he was forced to resign in 1777. He then became full-time MC at Brighton. His portrait, by Thomas Gainsborough, can be seen in the Great Octagon at the Assembly Rooms.

After Wade's departure it was decided to appoint separate Masters of Ceremonies for the Lower and Upper (New) Rooms. William Dawson became MC of the Upper Rooms in Bennett Street from 1777 to 1785 and Major William Brereton, an Irishman, held the post at the Lower Rooms from 1777 to 1780.

A noted soldier with the Inniskilling Dragoon Guards, Brereton had fought at Culloden in 1745. He resigned after three years and died in 1813 at the age of 89.

Richard Tyson succeeded Brereton at the Lower Rooms in 1780, and on Dawson's resignation five years later he took over at the Upper Rooms. James King then became MC at the Lower Rooms until 1805, when he succeeded Tyson at the New Rooms. He is mentioned by name in Jane Austen's *Northanger Abbey*. Both King and Tyson attempted to introduce new ideas and rules to the assemblies, but by their time Bath was already becoming less fashionable and attendances at functions were declining.

Bath's final Master of Ceremonies was Major Charles Simpson, who also served three times as the city's mayor. On his death in 1914 the post was discontinued.

The odd one out is Angelo Cyrus Bantam MC, who was the entirely fictitious creation of Charles Dickens, and appears in *The Pickwick Papers*. On Mr Samuel Pickwick's visit to the Rooms he is greeted effusively by Bantam ('Welcome to Ba-ath, sir. This is indeed an acquisition'), who welcomes him back to the city despite Pickwick's protestations that this is his first visit.

BRITAIN'S LAS VEGAS

In Georgian times the country was in the grip of gambling fever, and Bath, as England's most fashionable resort for high society, acted as a magnet for those who wished to court Lady Luck. Some were successful at the gaming tables, others less so. The stakes could be enormously high. Lady Mary Wortley Montagu, in a letter dated September 1725, reports that a certain Lady Lechmere had lost 'furious sums' at the tables, including £700 at one sitting (around £90,000 in today's values) and speculates on what her husband's reaction might be!

Among the most popular card and dice games of the day were Faro, Basset, Hazard and Ace of Hearts. Roulette, or 'Roly Poly' as it was often known, was also enjoyed by the gamesters. All this changed in 1739 when an Act of Parliament was passed which made all games of chance involving numbers illegal. New games were invented to circumvent the law, such as 'E.O.', which used letters instead of numbers, but these, too, met strong opposition from the anti-gaming lobby. The *Bath Chronicle* of January 1782 declared: 'The Keepers of these Destructive Traps for the Unwary are emancipated Felons.' The subsequent banning of such games effectively brought about the end of public gambling until modern times.

However, the wheel, it seems, is coming full circle (no pun intended!). At the time of writing, work has begun on the development of a casino and hotel in the Sawclose as part of a £19.7 million project due for completion in 2017.

SCANDALOUS BATH

Eighteenth-century Bath played host to a great variety of people and provided a fertile breeding-ground for gossip and scandal. Here is some that made the news at the time.

On 18 March 1772, the 18-year-old Elizabeth Ann Linley eloped from her home at No. 11 Royal Crescent with the young Irish playwright Richard Brinsley Sheridan. The Linleys were a highly regarded musical family, and Elizabeth, as well as being a noted beauty, was also an accomplished soprano. The young couple fled to France, but under pressure from Elizabeth's father, returned to England. A certain Captain Thomas Mathews, a married man and former suitor of Elizabeth's, then publicly insulted Sheridan and the two men duelled twice. On the first

occasion Mathews submitted, and on the second, which took place on Claverton Down, both men were wounded – Sheridan severely. After his recovery, he and Elizabeth were married and within the next five years he had penned his two famous plays: *The Rivals* and *The School for Scandal*.

In 1832 an 11-year-old girl named Marie Dolores Eliza Rosanna Gilbert, the daughter of an army officer and an Irish gentlewoman, arrived in Bath to further her education. At the age of 16 she eloped with an army lieutenant, but the marriage lasted only five years. She then became a professional dancer, assuming the name 'Lola Montez'. Adopting the life of a courtesan, she became the mistress of King Ludwig I of Bavaria, who gave her the title of Countess of Landsfeld. After a failed second marriage she toured Australia and also the USA, where she died in 1861. She is buried in Brooklyn.

In 1769 Evelyn Pierrepont, 2nd Duke of Kingston (after whom Pierrepont Street is named), married Elizabeth Chudleigh, a colonel's daughter who was a maid of honour to the Princess of Wales. Unfortunately, Elizabeth had been previously married to a naval officer and they had never been divorced. She was tried in the House of Lords for the crime of bigamy and found guilty. The penalty was branding, but she was excused this on the grounds of her title. After the trial she fled to France, dying in Paris in 1788.

For a short period in 1796, No. 1 Royal Crescent was leased by Frederick Augustus, Duke of York (the second son of George III). The duke was appointed commander-in-chief of the army, and in 1809 became involved in a scandal when his mistress, an actress named Mary Anne Clarke, was accused of procuring promotions for army officers, using the duke's name. After a lengthy public enquiry he was exonerated from blame but lost his command. His reputation never recovered and he is today chiefly remembered as the 'Grand Old Duke of York' in the children's rhyme.

The great Beau Nash himself was not immune from scandal, as we have already seen. At different times he kept at least four mistresses. The first of his best-known 'live-in' mistresses was

Frances 'Fanny' Murray (1729–78). According to her own account, she became involved with Nash when she was 14, living with him for several years before moving to London. There she became a noted prostitute and was subsequently the mistress of several prominent men, including Lord Sandwich. She was also involved with the debaucheries of the notorious Hellfire Club (a club for high-society rakes who met at Medmenham Abbey in Buckinghamshire for the practice of various immoral acts). Eventually she settled into a happy marriage with David Ross, a Scottish actor, with whom she remained until her death. She is believed to have inspired the character of Fanny Hill in John Cleland's 1748 novel.

Nash's other well-known mistress was Juliana Popjoy (1714–77), the daughter of a Wiltshire innkeeper. She became a dressmaker in Bath and had entered Nash's household by the year 1740. She gained the local nickname of 'Lady Betty Besom' from her habit of carrying a many-thonged whip as she rode around the city. When Nash's fortunes declined he was obliged to leave St John's Court and move into a smaller house nearby, which in modern times became a restaurant known as 'Popjoy's (it is now an Italian restaurant called the 'Amarone'). This establishment, and the neighbouring Theatre Royal, have been the locations for many sightings of the 'Grey Lady', a ghost thought by some to be that of Juliana.

In 1799 Mrs Jane Leigh Perrot, aunt to Jane Austen, was accused of shoplifting in Bath. While out walking with her husband she called into a haberdasherr's shop where she purchased a card of black lace, which was wrapped for her by an assistant. Passing the shop again on their return they were accosted by the shopkeeper, who accused Mrs Leigh Perrot of theft. When the parcel was opened, two lengths of lace were found. Charges were preferred and the unfortunate lady was committed for trial at Taunton. If found guilty, she was likely to have faced transportation. In the event, however, the jury quickly returned a verdict of 'not guilty' and she was acquitted. It was later supposed that the whole business was engineered by the shop in an attempt to coerce money from the Leigh Perrots so as to avoid a scandal.

Mary Robinson was born Mary Darby in Bristol in 1757 and was married at 15 to Thomas Robinson, by whom she had a daughter. When the child died, the couple moved to Bath, where Thomas's gambling led them into serious debt. One of his creditors, George Brereton, offered to cancel the debt if Mary would sleep with him! The marriage ended soon afterwards. She then embarked on a theatrical career, and had a succession of lovers who included the Prince of Wales. Eventually, ill health and a miscarriage led to her returning to Bath, where she took up writing and became a successful novelist. She died, aged 43, in 1800.

A VERY PRESTIGIOUS ADDRESS

Bath's famous Royal Crescent, built between 1767 and 1775, was conceived by John Wood the Elder and executed by his son (another John) after his father's death. Considered by many to be the peak of architectural achievement in the city, it has been home to a number of notable and eccentric residents.

Christopher Anstey (1724–1805): A country squire from Cambridgeshire, Anstey came to live in Bath in 1770, after several visits to take the waters. He lived for the rest of his life at No. 4, although the plaque recording his tenancy is (incorrectly) located on the wall of No. 5. He is best remembered as the author of *The New Bath Guide*, a lengthy satirical poem which pokes fun at the antics of fashionable society in Bath in the mid-eighteenth century. The book became a bestseller and there is a plaque to the author in Poet's Corner, Westminster Abbey.

Frederick Augustus, Duke of York (1763–1827): The second son of George III, he stayed for a while in 1796 at No. 1. He is 'The Grand Old Duke of York' of the nursery rhyme. He had a rather undistinguished military career, which was marred by a scandal in which his mistress was accused of taking bribes to secure (through

Frederick) promotions for army officers. Although himself exonerated, he was relieved of his command. On future visits he lodged at No. 16, now the Royal Crescent Hotel.

Jean Baptiste, Vicomte du Barré (1749–78): A French nobleman and gambler (said to be a relative of the famous Madame Dubarry, mistress of Louis XV), he lived at No. 8, where he held high-staked card parties. One November evening, after a quarrel with his gaming partner, Captain Rice, over how they should split the £650 they had won, they decided to settle the matter with pistols the following morning on Claverton Down outside the city. Du Barré was mortally wounded and was carried down to the George Inn, where he died. He is buried in the nearby churchyard of St Nicholas, Bathampton, where his grave can be seen. Rice was subsequently tried but acquitted of unlawful killing and went to Spain.

Princess Maria Thérèse de Lamballe (1749–92): A lady-in-waiting to Queen Marie Antoinette, she also lodged at No. 1 when she visited Bath in 1786. She seems to have been a considerable hypochondriac. The slightest shock would send her into a nervous collapse which could last for hours; the scent of violets made her extremely ill and the sight of shellfish (even in a picture) caused her to faint. She returned to France but, along with many other aristocrats, was murdered in September 1792 during the Revolution's Reign of Terror.

Elizabeth Ann Linley (1754–92): A soprano with an exceptional voice, Linley was also a noted beauty. Her father was Thomas Linley, composer and Director of Music in Bath, and the family lived at No. 11. It was from there that Elizabeth eloped in March 1772 with the young Irish playwright Richard Brinsley Sheridan. After their return to England, Sheridan fought two duels against one of Elizabeth's former suitors who had insulted him. Both sets of parents were opposed to the union and it was not until 1773 that they were finally married in London, where they subsequently lived. Sheridan went on to achieve great success with such plays as *The Rivals* and *The School for Scandal*. Elizabeth died of tuberculosis at the age of 38 and is buried in Wells Cathedral.

Lady Celia Noble (1870–1962): A granddaughter of the great Victorian engineer Isambard Kingdom Brunel, she lived at No. 22, after moving to Bath from London. Well-known as a patron of the arts, she moved in musical and artistic circles, and after coming to Bath, held concerts of chamber music at her house in the Crescent for many years. Mary, George V's Queen, visited her often during the Second World War. The last of the great society hostesses, Lady Noble died at the age of 92.

Sir Isaac Pitman (1813–97): The inventor or Pitman's Shorthand (or 'Stenographic Sound-hand', as it was originally known) lived at No. 17. He also created a Phonetic Alphabet, with which he hoped to transform English spelling. For most of his life he was a teetotaller, vegetarian, non-smoker and anti-vaccinationist. When a visitor to his house asked him which room was his study, he replied, 'I do not study – I only work!' He died at home at the age of 84 and there is a memorial to him in Bath Abbey.

Fanny Sage (*c.* 1762–1835): A noted beauty and an accomplished singer and player of the harpsichord, she gained the nickname of 'The Queen of Bath'. Her portrait was painted by George Romney. She lived in the Crescent for ten years but died, in relative obscurity, in France.

Philip Thicknesse (1719–92): This former soldier moved with his third wife to Bath in 1768, taking up residence at No. 9. An irascible and aggressive man, he seems to have been constantly at odds with his neighbours. He penned *The New Prose Bath Guide*, with which he hoped to rival Christopher Anstey's popular work, but it was not a success. However, he was instrumental in persuading the young Thomas Gainsborough to come to Bath, where he achieved great success. Thicknesse died at the age of 73 while on a visit to Boulogne.

It is not known for certain who had the longest tenancy in the Crescent, but we do know who had the shortest stay. That honour must surely belong to Mary Ellen, Countess of Berkeley, who moved into No. 21 late in the April of 1942. The following day, the Luftwaffe began its 'Baedeker' bombing raids on Bath. The poor lady spent that night in the basement of her new home and the next morning she moved out – for good!

SOME INTERESTING BATH PUBS

For many centuries Bath has been offering hospitality to its residents and visitors alike. Here is a selection of interesting hostelries:

Coeur de Lion, Northumberland Place: This lays claim to being Bath's smallest pub, and is believed to be the only pub of this name in the country. The origin of the name is uncertain. In the eighteenth century the building was known as Marchant's Court. The pub is owned by Abbey Ales, Bath's only brewery.

The Crystal Palace, Abbey Green: A seventeenth-century building which was once a lodging-house called The Three Tuns. According to local tradition, Lord Nelson once stayed here. It later became an inn and gained its present name at the time of the Great Exhibition of 1851. In the 1980s several skeletons and a Roman mosaic were uncovered in the cellar.

The Grapes, Westgate Street: This seventeenth-century building has an eighteenth-century frontage and became a pub (originally 'The Bunch of Grapes') in about 1800. It contains some fine Jacobean plasterwork. There are records of an earlier building on this site dating from the early 1300s.

The Huntsman, Terrace Walk: Built in the mid-1700s and probably designed by the architect John Wood the Elder, this is a Grade II* listed building. It was formerly a shop with a house attached and is believed to have the earliest surviving shopfront in the city.

The Old Green Tree, Green Street: This is another of Bath's older pubs, having been an inn since the 1770s. Originally it was only one room deep and had its own brewery. The 'Tree' is a very traditional pub with small, oak-panelled rooms.

The Pulteney Arms, Daniel Street: Popular with rugby fans, this pub is over 200 years old and close to the spectacular Great Pulteney Street. It regularly features in the CAMRA Good Beer Guide.

The Saracen's Head, Broad Street: Dating from around 1700, this was once a bookshop before becoming an inn where the young Charles Dickens stayed when he came to Bath as a Parliamentary reporter. While in the city he spotted the name 'Pickwick' (the name of a local coach proprietor) and adopted it as the name of the hero of his first novel.

The Volunteer Rifleman's Arms, New Bond Street Place: This small pub contains a collection of military memorabilia and photographs. It dates from the mid-1800s, when it was known simply as the Rifleman's Arms.

Sam Weller's, Upper Borough Walls: Named after Mr Pickwick's irrepressible manservant, this is a traditional pub/restaurant in the heart of the city.

BEING POOR IN BATH

There was plenty of accommodation in Bath for the well-to-do, but where could you go if you were destitute? Bath had a number of workhouses, some of which flourished until well into the twentieth century.

The Bath Union Workhouse, the city's largest, was built in 1836–38 on a site at Odd Down. It could accommodate more than 600 people and had 5 acres of vegetable gardens, orchards and a pigsty. Its chapel was dedicated to St Martin, who (according to legend) gave half his cloak to a beggar. This chapel, begun in 1846, was built by an inmate of the workhouse, one John Plass, who at the time was 78 years old.

In 1857 the manager of the Theatre Royal invited the workhouse children to a free performance of the pantomime, but when they arrived they were turned away. The workhouse guardians had changed their minds and decided that they did not want the children to be exposed to 'the habits of early dissipation'!

In 1881 the Master of the Workhouse was one George Dowling, with his wife, Elizabeth, as the Matron. The age range of the inmates varied from 1 to 90 years. In 1948, the buildings became St Martin's Hospital, as they still are today.

The Walcot Parish Workhouse stood alongside the London road and the building (rebuilt in the 1820s) is used today as retail premises. In 1837 a man named Withers was passing through Bath en route for London when he was taken ill and spent six weeks in this workhouse. The workhouse authorities then decided he should be removed to Clerkenwell, but by the time he arrived he was a total invalid. A court decided that his removal from Bath had been illegal and ordered that he be returned there so that he could be correctly processed and then returned to London! The parish of Walcot had to pay the legal expenses (£500) and also the cost of his keep while in London.

Batheaston also had a Parish Workhouse, or 'Poor House', built in 1821. However, in 1836 the inmates were transferred to the new Union Workhouse at Odd Down.

Bath has two surviving sets of almshouses:

St John's Hospital was founded around 1174 by Bishop Reginald FitzJocelin and is one of the oldest almshouses in England. It was built close to one of the city's hot springs so that its residents could benefit from the waters. The hospital was rebuilt in the eighteenth century, largely to the design of the elder John Wood. Today it provides homes for over 100 elderly local people and makes grants to various organisations in the city.

Partis College was built between 1825–27. It takes its name from the founders, Ann and Fletcher Partis, who wished to provide aid and accommodation for women left 'in reduced circumstances'. It contains thirty terraced houses, together with a chapel, and provides homes for women over 50 who are members of the Church of England. It stands on Newbridge Hill.

11

CEREMONIAL AND SPORTING BATH

BATH'S REGALIA

Bath's civic regalia consist of a sword, two maces, the city watch staves and the robes of office of the mayor and civic officials.

The Sword
Also known as the 'Bladud Sword', it is a double-edged, two-handed sword, 5ft 4in (162cm) long and weighing 7½lb (3.4kg). It is borne by the City Sword Bearer on civic occasions. The sword in use today is a copy, made by Wilkinson's of Pall Mall in 1902. The original sword was discovered in a barn at Swainswick, near Bath, and was lent to the city, but was later reclaimed by Oriel College, Oxford, who originally owned the property on which it was found. It currently hangs in the Great Hall at Oriel.

The Maces
These were made in London in 1708 by goldsmith Benjamin Pyne. They are silver gilt and are 45in (114cm) long. They are carried by two sergeants at mace, who accompany the mayor. They represent civic authority and are engraved with the city arms.

The City Watch Staves
These were made by Thomas Boddely in 1732 and contain both the Royal Arms and those of the City of Bath. The job of the City

Watch was originally to patrol the streets at night in order to keep the peace. They now accompany the mayor on civic occasions.

The Robes

Eighteenth-century mayors of Bath wore simple black gowns like those worn by undergraduates. However, it is likely that in Tudor times mayors wore scarlet and this custom was reintroduced in 1850.

The annual Mayor Making ceremony is held in Bath Abbey each June. The new mayor is elected by the Charter Trustees of the City of Bath and the civic leaders process in their robes from the Guildhall to the abbey, where the new mayor is officially installed. The first recorded mayor of Bath was John de Porta in 1230, and the present mayor (2017) is the 789th to hold the position. Notable former mayors of Bath have included the entrepreneur and stone mine owner Ralph Allen of Prior Park (1742), John Palmer, theatre owner and businessman (1796 and 1809), Eleazer Pickwick, landlord of the White Hart Inn (1826), whose surname was adopted by Charles Dickens for the hero of his famous novel, and Simon Barrow (1837), Bath's first Jewish mayor.

BATH'S COAT OF ARMS

The city's coat of arms, which probably dates from the sixteenth century, depicts a shield supported by a lion and a bear. The lion stands for royalty and bravery, the bear for ferocity and protection. They are standing on oak branches with acorns, which refer to the legend of King Bladud. Both creatures display crossed keys and sword, representing St Peter and St Paul, the patron saints of Bath Abbey. The shield they are holding displays the town wall surmounted by water, which represents both the river Avon and the mineral springs. Superimposed on these is the

sword of St Paul. Above the shield is a knight's helmet, indicating a municipality, and above that, the crown of King Edgar, which is being lifted by the arms of St Dunstan who performed the coronation ceremony. Beneath the shield is the motto 'Aquae Sulis' – the Roman name for Bath.

FLYING THE FLAG

Each year there are more than thirty days on which particular flags are flown from the flagstaff on the Guildhall to mark special occasions. As well as the Union flag you might see the United Nations flag, the Bath City flag, the White Ensign or the flags of various countries. Occasions which are marked in this way include Royal birthdays, St George's Day, Coronation Day, Commonwealth Day and the national days of countries with which Bath has an association, such as France, Germany, Hungary, the Netherlands and Australia.

PAGEANTRY IN ACTION

In 1909 Bath held a hugely ambitious Historical Pageant, which ran from 19 to 24 July. The president of the Pageant Committee was the Marquess of Bath, as Lord Lieutenant of the county of Somerset, and the patrons included Princess Louise and several members of the aristocracy. The pageant comprised eight famous episodes from the city's history, in the form of short plays, depicting such events as the coronation of King Edgar in AD 973, the visit of Queen Elizabeth I in 1590 and the Battle of Lansdown in 1643. The performances took place in Royal Victoria Park and involved over 3,000 players, most of whom had never acted before. The pageant was advertised as 'embracing all sects, all politics and all classes', and was the highlight of the city's year. Homage was also paid to literary characters and celebrities associated with Bath, with 'appearances' by authors such as Chaucer, Henry Fielding, Jane Austen and Charles Dickens, along with characters from some of their literary creations. The closing ceremony included a tableau with a 'stars and stripes' theme, in which ladies in Statue of Liberty costumes from towns named Bath across the USA and Canada gathered around 'Mother Bath'. There is a bronze plaque commemorating the whole event in Sydney Gardens.

NOTABLE BATH MPS

Bath has been represented in Parliament since 1386, when one Sewal Fraunceys was elected MP for the city. Other notable people who have held the post, together with their dates of tenure, are:

Sir Ralph Hopton (1625–26): A Royalist commander during the English Civil War, he fought at the Battle of Lansdown in 1643.

Robert Gay (1720–22): An eminent doctor and Fellow of the Royal Society, he owned land in Bath and gave his name to Gay Street.

George Wade (1722–47): Field Marshal and Commander-in-Chief during the 1745 Jacobite Rising, he had a house in Abbey Churchyard.

William Pitt the Elder (1757–63): He twice served as Prime Minister of Great Britain and for a time he owned No. 7 The Circus.

John Palmer (1801–07): Theatre owner and instigator of the countrywide mail coach system.

Sir James Pitman (1945–64): The grandson of Sir Isaac and inventor of the Initial Teaching Alphabet.

Christopher ('Chris') Patten (1979–92): Former Governor of Hong Kong and ex-Chairman of the BBC Trust, he lost his seat to Don Foster in 1992 and became Baron Patten of Barnes in 2005.

Donald ('Don') Foster (1992–2015): Former Liberal Democrat Chief Whip, he stood down from Parliament in 2015 and was created Baron Foster of Bath.

THIS SPORTING LIFE

Bath enjoys playing a part in the world of sports.

Rugby Union

Bath Rugby Club, one of the oldest in the country, was founded in 1865 as Bath Football Club and played mostly against local opposition, their first overseas tour being in 1954. They adopted the name 'Bath Rugby' upon turning professional in 1996. Well-known players produced by the club have included Jeremy Guscott and Phil de Glanville. Bath RC currently plays in the Aviva Premiership League. Like its neighbouring club in Bristol, it does not have a nickname. There is also an amateur team in the city called Bath Saracens RC.

Association Football

Bath City Football Club was formed in 1889 and currently plays in the Conference South League. It is a semi-professional club whose home ground is at Twerton Park in a suburb of Bath. The University of Bath also has its own clubs for soccer and futsal (a type of five-a-side football, usually played indoors).

Cricket

Bath Cricket Club was founded in 1859. It is an amateur club and runs four men's and two women's teams. Their home ground is on North Parade and they play in the West of England Premier League, where they have consistently been the most successful team.

Horse racing

The famous Bath Racecourse is situated on Lansdown Hill, just outside the city, and is the highest flat racecourse in Britain. The course is for thoroughbreds, and is 1 mile 4 furlongs in length. The first recorded horse race in Bath took place in 1728. During the Second World War the course was used by the RAF as a landing field.

Tennis

Bath has a number of tennis clubs, both indoor and outdoor. The Lansdown Club provides facilities for tennis, squash, racketball and croquet. The Bristol and Bath Tennis Club, founded in 1985, provides an opportunity for people to play Real Tennis (although it is located in Bristol).

Golf

Bath Golf Club, established in 1880, is one of the oldest inland courses in England. It is situated on Bathampton Down, near the folly known as Sham Castle. There is another 18-hole course on Lansdown and an Approach Golf course in Royal Victoria Park.

Olympic sports

The University of Bath on Claverton Down has superb facilities for many sports and has been a training ground for a number of Olympic and Paralympic athletes, competing under the TeamBath logo. These have included Amy Williams and Lizzy Yarnold (skeleton bobsleigh), Mark Foster (swimming), Kelly Gallagher (Alpine skiing) and Kate Howey (judo).

And ... anyone for boules?

Each year, in June, teams compete against each other in the very French game of boules, or petanque. This event, which is held in support of local charities, is played on the specially laid-out courts in the centre of Queen Square. Each team consists of a minimum of three players and contestants are encouraged to dress up. The 2015 event raised £44,000 for local charities.

The Bath Half Marathon

This has been held every year since 1981, usually on the second or third Sunday in March. The race is run around the streets of the city, covering a distance of 13.1 miles (21.1km) Over the years the race has raised millions of pounds for local, regional, national and international charities. A new event, the Bristol to Bath Marathon, was held for the first time in October 2015. This was the first inter-city marathon to take place in Britain and is planned to be an annual event.

Bike Bath

Bike Bath is an annual even consisting of cycle rides of 25, 50 or 80 miles, based on the centre of Bath and taking in the surrounding countryside.

12

IN THE STREET

STREET FURNITURE IN BATH

When walking around Bath, numerous items of 'street furniture' can be seen, which give clues about life in bygone times.

In Alfred Street, opposite the Assembly Rooms, stands No. 14, a house with several interesting pieces of street furniture. Straddling the gateway is a wrought-iron 'overthrow', containing a holder for a lamp. There are a number of these around the city, dating from the days when there was no street lighting in Bath and an oil lamp could be placed outside the house to light the entrance.

On either side of the gate are fine examples of 'link snuffers'. These iron cones provided a means of extinguishing the links, or burning torches, which were carried through the streets, usually by young boys, who would light the way for pedestrians after dark. With no street lighting, the 'link boy' would precede them to their door, then snuff out his torch when they were safely inside. Other examples can be seen around the city.

Also alongside the steps is a curious wrought-iron winch or windlass. This house has no steps leading down into the area outside the basement and the apparatus was used for lowering items which were being delivered to the tradesmen's entrance.

Many houses in the city have iron foot-scrapers by their front doors. When the streets and footpaths were muddy, visitors could scrape the dirt from their shoes before entering the house.

In Laura Place, at the end of Great Pulteney Street, is a fine example of a type of postbox known as a 'Penfold Hexagonal'. These were designed by an architect, John W. Penfold, and were made in Dudley between 1866 and 1879. There is another one farther along Great Pulteney Street.

Also in Great Pulteney Street, on either side, is a row of handsome replica nineteenth-century gas lamps (powered by electricity), installed for the filming of Thackeray's *Vanity Fair* in 2003. They replaced the modern streetlights and were left by the film company as a gift to the city when filming was complete.

At various locations in Bath can be seen examples of coalhole covers, some dating from the Georgian period. These hatches in the pavement gave access to the coal cellars in the basements of the houses. Coal could be delivered by simply lifting the cover and dropping the coal through. Some of these covers are round, some square or rectangular, and some are made of cast iron, while the older ones are of stone. Fine examples can be seen in Duke Street and Henrietta Street, while some in Cavendish Place have grooves to prevent rainwater from flowing into the cellars beneath.

A few examples of horse troughs still exist in Bath. There is a particularly fine one in Walcot Street, made from a variety of different types of stone. These troughs were an important feature of Georgian and Victorian Bath when the horse was the all-important means of transport and needed regular refreshment.

Flanking the entrance to the Holburne Museum in Sydney Place are what appear to be two stone sentry boxes. These are fine examples of 'watchmen's boxes' and date from the early nineteenth century. Before the creation of an official police force, local parishes would employ watchmen whose job was to patrol the streets at night and keep the peace. They could use the box to rest between patrols or as shelter in bad weather. There is another good example in Norfolk Crescent.

In the Georgian period wrought-iron railings were erected in front of all houses that had a basement area, to prevent people from falling in and also as a deterrent to intruders. The tops of the vertical bars (the 'finials') could be worked by the blacksmith into a variety of decorative shapes. Unlike many of the railings that surrounded parks and level areas, those protecting basements were not removed for scrap during the Second World War because of the danger to pedestrians during the blackout.

WINDOWS OF BATH

If windows are the 'eyes' of a building, then Bath has some interesting ones. Many houses in Bath display what are known as 'Venetian windows', which are in three sections, with the central panel having an arch over it and narrower side panes with flat tops. Despite its name, and the fact that it was first described by an Italian architect, Sebastian Serlio, you are unlikely to encounter any examples in Venice!

On the north side of Beauford Square, opposite the façade of the Theatre Royal, is a modest terrace of houses built in the early 1730s and designed by the Bristol architect John Strahan. Some of the windows in the houses are grouped in pairs; in fact,

you can see where, in some cases, individual windows have been moved closer together. This was done in an attempt to reduce Window Tax, which taxed homeowners according to the number of windows their homes had. The tax stipulated that windows which were not more than 12in (30cm) apart could be counted as a single window. The Window Tax was imposed between 1696 and 1851, when it was replaced by an 'inhabited house duty'. Many houses show blocked-in windows, which was also done to reduce the amount of Window Tax payable, although a 'dummy' window would sometimes be included for purposes of symmetry.

At the corner of Argyle Street and Grove Street, on the side wall of the Pulteney Bridge Restaurant, there is a *'trompe l'oeil'* showing a man sitting in a window, reading a book. This is so cleverly painted that most people do not even spot the deception. The building was once a bookshop and the painting was done in 1994 by Faulkner and Richards. It depicts the author Mowbray Green (1864–1945) reviewing his book on the architecture of Bath.

The great East Window in Bath Abbey contains 817 sq. ft (76m²) of stained glass depicting scenes from the life of Jesus. The window was partly blown in during the Bath Blitz of 1942, but was restored after the war by the great-grandson of the original designer.

Also in the abbey, to the left of the East Window, is the Edgar Window. This was installed in 1949 and shows the coronation of King Edgar in AD 973. The crown is being placed on his head by Dunstan, Archbishop of Canterbury.

Georgian sash windows can often be roughly dated from their style. Earlier ones tended to have smaller panes, usually with nine in each sash (sometimes known as 'nine over nine'), and with thicker wooden glazing bars. With improvements in glass technology, later windows could have larger (and therefore, fewer) panes, often showing a 'six over six' arrangement with thinner glazing bars.

Some of the pre-Georgian buildings still display the old stone-mullioned windows of the sixteenth and seventeenth centuries. Some also have the Cotswold-type 'dripstones' above the window

– a relic of the days before downpipes. Some good examples can be seen in the area around Abbey Green.

A tradition in Bath for many years has been to place a single lighted candle in each window of the houses in the Royal Crescent, The Circus and nearby streets at dusk on the evening of the opening of the annual Bath Festival.

... AND THE SMOKE GOES UP THE CHIMNEY JUST THE SAME

Chimneys of all sizes form a dominant feature of Bath's skyline. Here are some notable ones:

Behind the parapet on the roof of the Guildhall, above a false window, is a chimney designed to look like a sacrificial altar and draped with garlands. The architect was Thomas Baldwin and the building dates from the mid-1770s.

The rows of chimney pots, especially in the larger houses such as those in the Royal Crescent, give a clue to the large number of fireplaces, and therefore rooms, that the buildings contained.

The tall, Classical-style chimney visible behind the buildings in York Street belongs to the old Bath City Laundry in Swallow

Street. This building was designed by Major Charles Davis and opened in the 1880s.

Another Classically inspired chimney can be seen above the Cross Bath at the end of Beau Street. In Victorian times this bath was known as the 'Tuppenny Hot'. The original eighteenth-century design was by Baldwin, with features like the chimney being subsequently added by John Palmer (the architect, not the timeshare fraudster!)

Alongside the Kennet and Avon Canal in Widcombe stands the Pumphouse Chimney. Originally constructed in the 1840s, the 30ft chimney gradually developed a two-degree lean and this was recreated when it was restored in 2011. The chimney was originally part of one of the pumphouses that were used to pump water from the Avon to keep the canal topped up. It was built in a very ornate style for the benefit of wealthy residents who would not have appreciated the view of an 'industrial' style chimney.

Beside Widcombe Lock on the canal, near where it links to the Avon, can be seen Thimble Mill, with its tall, square chimney. This once housed a steam pump which pumped water uphill to replace the 50,000 gallons (227,000l) which were lost each time a boat passed through the locks.

Not strictly a chimney, but the large stone cylindrical structure amid the greenery next to the Hilton Hotel in Walcot Street is a ventilation shaft for the underground car park. It replaced a previous version from the 1960s which was huge, slab-sided and unbelievably ugly.

SOME STRANGE BATH SIGNS

Beneath the pediment of the Pump Room is the Greek inscription 'ΑΡΙΣΤΟΝ ΜΕΝ Υ'ΔΩΡ', which is taken from the works of Pindar and roughly translates as 'Water is Best'. This also appears (in English) beneath the statue of Rebecca which stands to the north of the abbey, and was (not surprisingly) placed there by the Bath Temperance Society in 1861.

To the south of the abbey stands Kingston Buildings. Its name, carved in the stonework of the side wall, is in the Phonetic Alphabet devised by Sir Isaac Pitman, who lived in Bath. His 'Phonetic Institute' once occupied part of the building and his (unsuccessful) aim was to simplify English spelling.

On the wall of the nave in Bath Abbey is a 'tetragrammaton', a sign containing the four letters of the Hebrew title for God – YHWH. This is thought to have been carved by a Parliamentarian soldier during the English Civil War.

Under the statue on the wall of the Victoria Art Gallery is an inscription which some visitors (and locals) find puzzling – 'HIM Queen Victoria'. Not a gender issue; the letters stand for 'Her Imperial Majesty' (from the days when Britain had an empire!).

A pediment above a window of No. 22 Grove Street bears the odd date '5792'. This date might be a reference to the curious belief of Archbishop Ussher (1581–1656), who declared that the world was created in the year 4004 BC. 5792, therefore, would translate as 1788. Alternatively, the numbers might refer to the Masonic calendar, which begins at 4,000 BC. This would give a date of 1792.

Mallory, the jewellers in Bridge Street, has a sign which proclaims 'Watchmaker to the Admiralty'. Bath has a long-established connection with the navy, with Ministry of Defence contractors supplying a variety of services and equipment.

In Abbeygate Street, on the side wall of Marks and Spencer's store, is displayed the company's coat of arms, containing a representation of St Michael and a pair of scales to signify fair trading. Also shown is the M & S motto: 'Strive, Probe, Apply' (SPA). A happy coincidence of initials for Bath!

On one of the panels in the frieze above the Guildhall can be seen the initials of the city of Rome – SPQR. They stand for 'Senatus Populusque Romanus' (the Senate and People of Rome) – a reminder of Bath's Roman heritage.

Set into the paving stones of Abbey Churchyard is a circular plaque which marks one end of the Cotswold Way. This is a long-distance footpath which runs 102 miles (164km) from Bath to Chipping Campden in Gloucestershire.

On the wall of No. 48 Milsom Street (now Hobbs) can be seen two signs. One declares that the building was once a 'Circulating Library and Reading Room'; the other says 'State Lottery Office'. This was operated from this address from 1824 to 1830.

In Cheap Street, above the green door marked 'Shum's Court' can be seen (very faintly) the inscription 'Dill's Famous Bacon and Pork'. The Dill and Shum families, both butchers, carried out their operations from a courtyard behind these buildings. The two families later amalgamated their businesses.

ARCHITECTURAL ODDITIES

In Camden Crescent, the main pediment has a coat of arms containing three elephants' heads. This was the crest of Charles Pratt, 1st Earl Camden (1714–94), who served as Recorder of Bath from 1759 until his death. Also, supporting the pediment are five columns; correct architectural grammar decrees that there should be an even number, so that there is not a column immediately beneath the apex of the pediment. The keystones above the doorways also bear the elephant's head motif.

In Grove Street stands a Palladian building (now converted into flats) which was once a prison. Most unusually, the first floor has rustication (where the horizontal and vertical joints between the blocks are heavily emphasised). This is usually reserved for the ground floor, as it gives a feeling of solidity. There is a good reason for this departure from the norm. Like most Bath buildings the basement was originally sited at ground level, with the intention of later constructing the street on vaults, thereby bringing it to the level of what would then become the ground floor. However, this was never done, with the result that the basement remained as the ground floor, and the original 'front door' had to be changed into a window.

On the south side of Quiet Street stands the Royal Bank of Scotland, in an 1824 building that was formerly the Auction

Mart and Bazaar. On either side of the big, three-light first-floor window are two statues in niches. The one on the left represents 'Commerce'; the other (who appears to be scratching her stomach) stands for 'Genius'.

Two of the houses in North Parade Passage have oval apertures in their roof gables. These are 'owl holes' constructed to allow access for predatory birds such as barn owls (they were encouraged as a means of keeping down vermin such as rats and mice). No. 4 (Sally Lunn's) actually has a stone owl mounted in the opening; it can be seen if you stand well back.

In Royal Victoria Park, just past the entrance with the obelisk and the lions, is an attractive example of a '*cottage orné*' (that is, a cottage in a rustic style that is not related to real agriculture). This is Park Place Farm House, designed by Edward Davis and built in 1831.

On the fronts of some houses can be seen 'bressumer' beams. These are wooden beams that stretch across the face of the house just above ground-floor level and were usually lime-washed to blend with the stonework. Their purpose was to absorb any movement in the stonewall. They also had the advantage of allowing the ground floor front to be kept open during building to allow materials to be taken inside. A good example can be seen on the 'Bath Bun' teashop in Abbey Green.

Many of the Georgian street names can be seen carved into the stonework of the buildings – sometimes they were painted as well. These were done with great skill and care – in some cases, even down to the inclusion of full stops! Good examples can be seen in Upper Borough Walls and Pierrepont Street.

Parish boundary marks, also inscribed on the walls of buildings, have survived in some parts of Bath – for example, the one in Upper Borough Walls marking the boundary between St Michael and St Peter and Paul parishes. This was important in the days when each parish was a separate administrative unit with responsibility for the people who lived within it. The parish authorities had to deal with such matters as poor relief, road repairs and street lighting, the costs of which would be met from the local rates.

In Upper Borough Walls can be seen a short stretch of crenellated wall. This is all that remains of the medieval wall which once surrounded the city. The top part is a Victorian reconstruction.

Topping the balustrade above the upper storey of The Circus (where, if anything, one might expect to see pineapples) are modern copies of the original stone acorns, 108 in all. Why the elder John Wood chose this motif is not clear, but it might have been a nod to the Druids, the ancient British priesthood who venerated the oak tree and who, Wood believed, had a temple at or near Bath. Equally it could be a reference to the Prince Bladud legend, acorns being a food of pigs, which were, according to the story, the first to discover the healing powers of the springs (see 'Bathonians who never were').

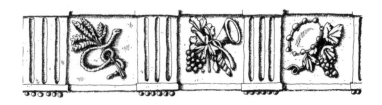

Also to be seen in The Circus, above the ground-floor windows, is a continuous stone frieze containing symbols representing the arts, trades, sciences and other images. Altogether there are more than 500.

On Claverton Down, and visible from Grand Parade, is Sham Castle, a folly built in 1762 by Richard Jones and probably to

a design by Sanderson Miller. Jones was Clerk of the Works to Ralph Allen and the 'castle' (which is merely a façade) was built as an 'eye-catcher', visible at the time from Allen's townhouse off York Street. It also provided work for some of the unemployed stonemasons in the city. At night it is floodlit.

By the side of the river, just south of North Parade Bridge, is a curious little stone-built shelter, or folly, known as 'Delia's Grotto'. It is here that Elizabeth Ann Linley and Richard Brinsley Sheridan are said to have left love-notes to each other, since both sets of parents were opposed to their liaison. The grotto may have been built as early as 1734 and was probably part of the eighteenth-century development known as 'Harrison's Walk'. Thomas Harrison was the owner of the Assembly Rooms which once stood on Grand Parade. No one seems to know who 'Delia' was, after whom the grotto is named.

In the grounds of No. 20 Lansdown Crescent, and visible from the Mews behind the Crescent, is a summerhouse built in an Islamic style, with a domed roof which used to be surmounted by the symbols of a crescent and a star.

In Somerset Place, next to Lansdown Crescent West, the keystones above the doors have a curious 'icicle mask' design.

The architect, John Eveleigh, also used this motif at Grosvenor Place, another of his achievements in Bath. Some have suggested that it was to commemorate the hard winter of 1790–91, when the construction of both projects was in progress.

On the east side of the river near Pulteney Bridge are the Beazer Gardens, named after the Bath-based construction company who donated the land. Here can be found the Beazer Maze, a paved stone maze with a mosaic representation of the Gorgon's head (from the Roman temple of Sulis Minerva) at its centre. Designed by Gilbert Coate and Adrian Fisher, the maze was unveiled in 1984 and is very popular with children. Incidentally, it is technically a labyrinth rather than a maze, as there is only one path to the centre. The origins of these go back to ancient times and may have represented Man's difficult pathway to God.

Spanning York Street is a decorative Classical archway linking the Roman Baths with the building opposite, which was formerly the Swallow Street laundry. This utilised hot water from the thermal springs and the archway conceals the pipe through which the water ran. At the time of writing the building contains workshops, but is due to be developed into a learning centre for the Roman Baths Museum.

A few buildings in the city have stumps of stone projecting from one side. These were intended to link to other houses or extensions which were never built. The Dispensary in Cleveland Place shows a good example of this.

'... FROM LITTLE ACORNS'

As we have noted, the acorns which adorn the parapets of the houses in The Circus are not the originals, but concrete replacements. In 1962 Brown Morton III, an American architectural student staying in Bath, spotted two of the originals being loaded on to a lorry, and offered to buy them. The builders refused, but added that they could not be responsible if he followed them and saw where they were dumped! He did so, salvaged them and took them back with him to South Carolina. They have since been shipped back to Bath and are now in the keeping of the Museum of Bath Architecture in The Paragon. They may well be the last of the original Circus acorns.

13

HEALTH AND EDUCATION

BATH HOSPITALS

Bath is home to several well-respected hospitals, some of which have been serving the needs of the community for many years.

The Royal United Hospital (or RUH): This major hospital was formed in 1828 with the amalgamation of Bath Casualty Hospital (1788) and the City Dispensary and Infirmary (1792). It was granted its 'Royal' prefix by Queen Victoria in 1864. Originally in Beau Street, it moved to its present location in Weston in 1932. An admin block is located in a former medieval manor house that was remodelled in the 1700s and given an Adam interior. In 2014 the hospital received confirmation of a five-year, £110 million development project.

St Martin's Hospital, Odd Down: Opened in 1838 as Bath Union Workhouse, this became a hospital in 1948, taking its name from the former Workhouse chapel which bore the saint's name.

The Royal National Hospital for Rheumatic Diseases: Originally opened in 1738 as the Mineral Water Hospital, it is still known affectionately by locals as 'The Min'. The building was designed, free of charge, by John Wood the Elder, and the stone for its building was donated by Ralph Allen. Funding was assisted by

Beau Nash, who raised subscriptions among wealthy visitors. In 1860 a further wing was added to the west. In early 2015 the hospital was absorbed into the RUH Bath NHS Foundation Trust.

DOCTOR, DOCTOR ...

Because of Bath's reputation as a centre of healing, many physicians, reputable and otherwise, set up their practices in the city. Here are some of the most well known:

Dr James McKittrick Adair (1728–1802): A Scot, Adair spent some years in the Caribbean before returning to Scotland and taking his medical degree in Edinburgh. In 1783 he settled in Bath, where he waged a campaign against charlatans in the medical profession, whom he described as 'quacks, mountebanks, gout doctors ... toad-eaters and puffing gossips'. He gave the proceeds from his published works to support the Bath Hospital.

Dr William Bowen (1761–1815): Bowen had a practice in Bath and was called in to treat Mrs Cassandra Austen (Jane's mother; then in her sixties) while the Austens were living at No. 4 Sydney Place. She recovered, and lived for another twenty years. She attributed her recovery to 'the skill and attention of Bowen'.

Dr George Cheyne (1671–1743): Cheyne was a Scotsman who set up a practice in Bath in 1702. A popular and colourful character, at one time he weighed about 32 stone (about 200kg), despite being a strict vegetarian. In 1724 he published *An Essay on Health and Long Life*, for which he became famous. His clients included poet Alexander Pope, playwright John Gay and Richard 'Beau' Nash.

Dr William Falconer (1744–1824): Formerly physician to Chester Infirmary, he came to Bath in 1770 and lived in The Circus. He practiced in the city for over fifty years, and from 1784 to 1819 was physician at the Bath General Hospital. He also initiated the planting of the five plane trees in The Circus. His son and grandson were both doctors who practised in Bath, and his grandson, Randle Wilbraham Falconer, was elected mayor in 1857.

Dr John Hunter (1728–93): Hunter was widely regarded as England's leading surgeon. In 1776 he was appointed Surgeon Extraordinary to King George III and also held the posts of Surgeon General and Inspector General of Hospitals. One of his pupils was Edward Jenner, the discoverer of vaccination against smallpox. Hunter lived and practiced for a time in Bath, but died of a heart attack after an argument at St George's Hospital, London, and is buried in Westminster Abbey.

Dr William Oliver (1695–1754): Oliver was a Cornishman who settled in Bath around 1725 and was later appointed principal physician at the Mineral Water Hospital shortly after it opened in 1739. He is widely remembered as the inventor of the 'Bath Oliver', a hard, dry biscuit given to his patients as part of a healthy diet. He became a Fellow of the Royal Society and is buried in All Saints' Church in the nearby village of Weston. He should not be confused with the Dr William Oliver (1659–1716), who is buried in Bath Abbey, where he has a commemorative plaque. A cousin, once removed, of the other Dr Oliver (and not, as some sources have suggested, his natural father), he was a surgeon with the Duke of Monmouth's army and later became Physician to the Royal Hospital at Greenwich.

Dr Caleb Hillier Parry (1755–1822): Gloucestershire-born Parry obtained his MD at Edinburgh. He came to Bath in 1779, where he became physician to the Bath General Hospital (later the Mineral Water Hospital). He prospered, and by the time he retired he was earning £3,000 per year. His large collection of books now forms part of the medical library at Bristol University. He was the father of the Arctic explorer William Edward Parry.

Dr Jeremiah 'Jerry' Peirce (1696–1768): Peirce became a governor of the Mineral Water Hospital, and was appointed as its senior surgeon on the same day that William Oliver became its physician. Like Oliver, he was a Fellow of the Royal Society. He lived in a small villa on Lansdown and is buried in St Swithin's church, Walcot.

Dr John Radcliffe (1652–1714): Radcliffe never practised in Bath, but worked for many years in London, where he became Royal Physician to William and Mary and subsequently to Queen Anne. The Radcliffe Infirmary in Oxford, the city in which he studied, is named after him. Radcliffe was very disparaging about Bath's 'water cure', which he saw as potentially damaging to the livelihood of metropolitan doctors, and threatened to poison the springs by casting toads into them. Beau Nash's response was to employ musicians to play in the adjacent Pump Room, so that they could, as he put it, 'fiddle the amphibian creatures out'.

Tobias George Smollett (1721–71): Scottish by birth, Smollett qualified as a surgeon at the University of Glasgow, and took his MD at Aberdeen. He lived for a short while in Bath, but his medical career always took second place to his writing, and he became a best-selling author, with novels such as *The Adventures of Roderick Random* and *The Adventures of Peregrine Pickle*. His last work, *The Expedition of Humphry Clinker*, is partly set in Bath.

Bath also attracted its quota of doctors whose qualifications were, at the very least, dubious. The term 'quack', when referring to a bogus doctor, is believed to be a shortened form of 'quacksalver'. This comes from an old Dutch word which originally meant someone using home remedies, but gradually came to mean a person employing false cures or suspect knowledge. There must have been numerous 'doctors' of this type operating in eighteenth-century Bath, where there was a good deal of money to be made in ministering to the needs, real or imaginary, of wealthy patients.

EDUCATION, EDUCATION …

Bath has always been keen to promote education and training for its citizens. Here are some examples:

Bath College is located in Avon Street in the heart of the city. A further education college, it was formed in 2015 by the merger of the City of Bath and Norton Radstock Colleges. The college started out in 1892 as a science, art and technical school, passing through a number of changes and amalgamations before reaching its present incarnation.

Bath Spa University is largely located on the Newton Park campus to the west of the city. This is leased from the Duchy of Cornwall and includes a Georgian mansion, currently used as an administration building. The university was previously a teacher-training college, then became, successively, the Bath College of Higher Education and Bath Spa University College, finally gaining full university status in 2005. The university also has campuses at Sion Hill, Bath, and Corsham in Wiltshire. Famous alumni include composer Sir Harrison Birtwistle, shoe designer Manolo Blahnik and cookery writer Mary Berry.

King Edward's School was founded in 1552 under laws passed during the reign of Henry VIII to create grammar schools to replace the old monastic schools. Originally located in Frog Lane (now New Bond Street), it moved to a new building in Broad

Street in the mid-1750s, where it remained until the 1960s, when it relocated to a new site at North Road. Today it is an independent school providing education for over 900 pupils between the ages of 3 and 19. At the time of writing, the eighteenth-century, Grade II* listed building in Broad Street is on the 'at risk' register, having been refused permission for its redevelopment as either a pub or a hotel.

Kingswood School was founded by the evangelist John Wesley and is the oldest Methodist educational institution in the world. It first opened in 1748 at Kingswood, near Bristol, and moved to its present location in 1851, keeping its former name. It was originally established to provide an education for the sons of Methodist clergy. Today it is independent and co-educational and has around 1,000 pupils between the ages of 3 and 18. Former pupils include the actors Tim Curry, Nicholas le Prevost and Emily Head, as well as two holders of the Victoria Cross.

Norland College is on the London Road east of the city. It provides training in childcare, and produces the famous 'Norland Nannies' and nursery nurses, employed throughout the world. The college was founded by Emily Ward in 1892.

Prior Park College is one of the foremost Roman Catholic boarding and day schools in the UK, with a complement of around 600 students. The college is housed in a Palladian mansion designed by John Wood I and completed in about 1750. It was originally the home of quarry owner and entrepreneur Ralph Allen, before becoming a seminary, a grammar school, and finally a co-educational, fee-paying college, open to all faiths. The adjoining 57-acre (23-hectare) landscape gardens were once part of the school grounds, but are now in the care of the National Trust. Notable former pupils include the theatrical producer Sir Cameron Mackintosh and Cormac Murphy-O'Connor, former Archbishop of Westminster.

Ralph Allen School stands on Combe Down and is a comprehensive school which achieved academy status in 2012. It is named after Ralph Allen of nearby Prior Park and opened in 1958. The school is a co-educational, non-denominational institution of about 1,000 students. It also provides facilities and venues for various activities and events in the community.

The University of Bath grew from a nineteenth-century technical school in Bristol, which rapidly expanded. No suitable site being available in Bristol, it relocated to a site at Claverton Down and received its Royal Charter in 1966. It occupies a high position in the university league tables and its sporting organisation, TeamBath, has helped to produce some of the UK's top Olympic athletes, including Amy Williams, gold medallist at the 2010 Winter Olympics. Currently, the university has around 16,000 students. In the year 2000 it opened a second campus in Swindon, Wiltshire.

The following well-known people are among those who have received honorary doctorates from the university:

Sir Peter Hall CBE, theatre director: Honorary Doctor of Letters.
Michael Eavis CBE, farmer/founder of the Glastonbury Festival: Honorary Doctor of Arts.
Sir Ian Botham OBE, cricketer: Honorary Doctor of Laws.
Mary Robinson, former President of the Republic of Ireland: Honorary Doctor of Laws.
Sir Terry Pratchett OBE, late author: Honorary Doctor of Letters.
James 'Midge' Ure OBE, musician: Honorary Doctor of Laws.

14

ON THIS DAY IN BATH

1 January 1825: The Rector of Camerton, the Revd John Skinner, attended a meeting in Bath to decide whether a local road should become a turnpike; i.e. a road on which tolls could be charged for its maintenance. However, the assembly was so badly run and so biased that he left in disgust, vowing never again to attend such a meeting.

2 January 1904: This was the date on which Bath saw its first electric trams operating. The Bath Electric Tramways Company fleet consisted of fifty-five cars painted in blue and yellow. The service continued to operate until 1939. Since then there have been several proposals for the re-introduction of a tram service in the city.

5 January 1842: Two large stones placed on the Great Western Railway line nearly caused a derailment 3 miles (5km) east of Bath. Fortunately the train was able to crush one and thrust the other aside. No one was seriously hurt, although the driver and stoker received superficial injuries.

9 January 1842: The *Morning Post* published a letter describing a disaster at Combe Down, in which a large area above a disused stone mine had subsided, causing the destruction of many properties and considerable loss of life. The letter proved to be a hoax.

11 January 1885: At Limpley Stoke, two railway labourers lost their lives when the stable in which they were sleeping was crushed under the weight of tons of stone that slid down the slope above. A new goods shed was being erected nearby and the loose stone had been piled up above the stable. As well as the two men, six horses were also killed.

13 January 2006: This day saw a celebratory service in Bath Abbey to mark the inauguration of Bath Spa University. The previous year the former college had been granted full university status. The Mayor of Bath led a procession from the Guildhall to the abbey.

15 January 1840: Frances 'Fanny' Burney (1752–1840), aka Madame D'Arblay, was buried at St Swithin's church, Walcot. A highly acclaimed novelist, she and her French soldier husband, Alexandre D'Arblay, had lived in Bath for three years until his death in 1818. She then moved to London, after which she ceased to write novels. On her death her body was returned to Bath to be interred alongside her husband.

19 January 1825: The Bath Royal Scientific and Literary Institution was ceremonially founded on this day and was officially opened to the public two days later. It then stood in Terrace Walk, before moving to its present location in Queen Square.

21 January 1766: The actor and bon viveur James Quin (1693–1766) died at his house in Bath, to which he had retired. Of Irish descent, he was most famous for his interpretation of Shakespeare's Sir John Falstaff. Quin is buried in Bath Abbey, where a plaque to his memory can be seen.

22 January 1897: Sir Isaac Pitman, inventor of Pitman's Shorthand, died on this day at his home in the Royal Crescent, where he had lived for over fifty years. He had also made a name as a printer, editor and publisher.

25 January 1991: After a £2 million restoration, the Assembly Rooms were reopened by the Duchess of Kent. Four years previously, the ballroom ceiling had collapsed. The rooms had previously suffered considerable damage in 1942 when the building was struck by incendiary bombs. They were restored and reopened in 1963.

27 January 1539: This was the sad day on which the head of Bath Abbey, Prior Holloway, signed the paper which surrendered the abbey to Henry VIII's commissioners. He was awarded a pension of £80 p.a., and the eighteen monks who made up the community also received pensions. At the time of its closure the abbey was the second richest in Somerset, the wealthiest being Glastonbury, which closed later the same year.

28 January 1933: The distinguished writer, scholar and critic George Edward Saintsbury, sometime Professor of English Literature at Edinburgh University, died at his home at No. 1a Royal Crescent. He coined the term 'Janeite' for fans of Jane Austen.

1 February 1945: Following the end of the war, plans were drawn up by Sir Patrick Abercrombie for the redevelopment of Bath and were presented to the city on this day. The plans included a new road network and the moving of the Council Offices to the Royal Crescent. Perhaps fortunately, the plans never got off the drawing board!

3 February 1761: On this day, Bath's most famous Master of Ceremonies, Richard 'Beau' Nash, died at his home in Sawclose, at the age of 86. His influence on the development of Bath as a pleasure resort was enormous and spread far beyond the confines of the city. His nickname of the 'King of Bath' was well deserved.

7 February 1754: The foundation stone of the first house in The Circus was laid. It was intended that the name of the development should be the King's Circus, with an equestrian statue of George II in the centre. Due to cost, the statue was never erected.

11 February 1768: On this day the foundation stone for the new Guildhall was laid by the Mayor of Bath. However, due to delays, the building was not completed for another ten years.

13 February 1829: A by-election was held in Bath, with only two candidates standing. They were George Pratt, Earl of Brecknock (Tory), and General Charles Palmer (Whig). The result was a dead heat, with all votes being declared valid. The election had to be re-run and this time the earl was declared the winner.

14 February 1951: The last train to use the Camerton Branch Line of the Bristol & North Somerset Railway ran on this day. The line opened in 1882 and was used as the setting for the 1953 Ealing comedy *The Titfield Thunderbolt*. The track was eventually taken up in 1958.

16 February 2003: The episode of Channel 4's *Time Team* series carrying out the first archaeological dig at the Royal Crescent was broadcast on this day. The dig took place on the open ground to the south of the Crescent. The team was looking for signs of Roman occupation and found evidence of a Roman road which may have been part of the Fosse Way which ran through Bath.

17 February 1761: This day saw the funeral of the great Beau Nash, which took place in Bath Abbey. Nash had served as the city's Master of Ceremonies for more than fifty years and became nationally famous as an arbiter of taste and fashion. Bath Corporation made a contribution of 50 guineas towards the funeral expenses.

19 February 1827: The Revd John Skinner, Rector of Claverton, was summoned to appear before Bath's Court of Requests for non-payment of a bill that was owed to one of his tenants. The court eventually found in Skinner's favour, even though he had been late for the hearing.

23 February 1936: Citizen House, a Georgian town house in the centre of Bath, was destroyed by fire. The house, originally built for the Duke of Chandos, caught fire during the evening and the blaze was reported in the *Bath and Wilts Chronicle* under the headline: 'HISTORIC BATH MANSION UTTERLY DESTROYED. WARDEN'S TWO CHILDREN RESCUED BY FIRE CHIEF'. In all, three people were rescued from the blazing building.

25 February 1728: John Wood the Younger was baptised in Bath Abbey on this day. Following in his father's footsteps he became an architect, working alongside the elder Wood and continuing their work after his father's death in 1754. Wood junior was responsible for the completion of The Circus, the Royal Crescent and the Upper Assembly Rooms, as well as other buildings elsewhere in the country.

27 February 1927: After exceptionally heavy rain, the river Avon rose more than 3ft (1m) overnight, resulting in severe flooding in Bath. The worst affected area was Dolemeads, in the southern part of the city. Many people had to be rescued by boat.

29 February 1928: The politician and lawyer George (Viscount) Cave (1856–1928) died in Bath on this day. A former Home Secretary and Lord Chancellor, he became ill and chose to undergo an operation in Bath, where he could recuperate afterwards. Unfortunately the surgery was not successful and he died a month later.

2 March 1950: As part of a three-day tour of the West Country, the 23-year-old Princess Elizabeth visited Bath. Large crowds turned out, despite the heavy rain. During her visit she opened the teacher-training college at Newton St Loe, which is part of the estate of the Duchy of Cornwall.

5 March 1979: The Theatre Royal, Sawclose, was purchased for £155,000 by a trust led by the entrepreneur Jeremy Fry, to be run as a non-profit making concern.

7 March 1820: The Bath architect Thomas Baldwin died on this day. In 1776 he was appointed City Architect and Surveyor and his works include the Guildhall, Bath Street and the Cross Bath, and much of Bathwick, across the river. In 1796 he was dismissed from his post after accusations of false accounting and was declared bankrupt. However, he still continued to practice, though not in Bath. He died at his home in Great Pulteney Street and is buried in St Michael's church, Broad Street.

11 March 1827: The architect John Pinch the Elder died in Bath on this day. He was responsible for designing some of the city's later Georgian buildings.

12 March 1984: This day saw the death of playwright and actor Arnold Ridley, probably best known for his role as Private Charles Godfrey in the television series *Dad's Army*. He was born in Bath in 1896 and served in the First World War before being discharged through injury. He began acting and writing, and his first play, *The Ghost Train* (1925), was a huge success. He wrote more than thirty others and continued to act in films and on radio. He was awarded an OBE in 1982 and is buried in Bath Abbey Cemetery.

13 March 1781: This was the date on which the astronomer William Herschel (1738–1822) discovered a hitherto unknown planet from his observatory at his house in New King Street, using a telescope he had built himself. He first thought to name the planet *Georgium Sidus* (George's Star) in honour of King George III, but it was eventually decided to name it Uranus, after Urania, the Greek goddess of astronomy.

17 March 1764: Dr William Oliver (1695–1764) died in Bath on this day. As chief physician at the Mineral Water Hospital he was responsible for the Bath Oliver, a dry biscuit he created as part of a healthy diet for his patients. Towards the end of his life he gave the recipe to his coachman, who set up a successful business. Dr Oliver is buried in the churchyard of All Saints, Weston, on the outskirts of Bath, where his family owned the Manor House.

18 March 1772: On the evening of this day Elizabeth Ann Linley and Richard Brinsley Sheridan eloped from her parents' house in the Royal Crescent. They went to London and took ship for France, where they underwent a marriage ceremony in Calais, before her father arrived and accompanied them back to Bath.

21 March 1793: This day saw the collapse of Bath City Bank, due largely to the effects of the Napoleonic War and the threat of invasion. Several of Bath's prominent citizens, including the architect Thomas Baldwin, were bankrupted.

23 March 1960: On this day Queen Elizabeth the Queen Mother visited the city to commemorate the conclusion of the £100,000 restoration of Bath Abbey. She also opened a college of domestic science at Sion Hill. Thousands of schoolchildren were given time off from school and lined the route.

24 March 1935: On this day the cookery writer and broadcaster Mary Berry CBE was born in the city. After studying catering at Bath College of Domestic Science she completed a course at Le Cordon Bleu School in France. She has written more than seventy cookery books and has hosted a number of television programmes, including *The Great British Bake Off*.

27 March 1994: Demonstrators gathered in Laura Place at the end of Great Pulteney Street to protest against the building of the Batheaston Bypass. A protest camp was set up on Solsbury Hill, near the proposed route, which was to run through attractive scenery to the east of the city. The protest was unsuccessful and the bypass was completed in the summer of 1996.

28 March 1828: Frances Burney (1776–1828), niece of the acclaimed novelist Frances 'Fanny' Burney, died at her mother's house in King Street. During her life she worked as a governess and also wrote plays, but never achieved the fame of her aunt. She died from jaundice and is buried at Batheaston church.

1 April 1974: This was the day on which, under government boundary changes, the County of Avon came into being. Bath was assimilated, along with Bristol and parts of north Somerset and south Gloucestershire. The move was not generally popular, and on the same date in 1996 the county of Avon was abolished and the unitary authority of Bath and North East Somerset was formed.

4 April 1802: This day saw the death, in Bath, of Lloyd Kenyon, 1st Baron Kenyon (1732–1802). A prominent politician and barrister, he served as Master of the Rolls, Attorney General and Lord Chief Justice of England. Though highly learned in law, his grasp of Latin was uncertain, which led George III to remark: 'My Lord, it would be well if you would stick to your good law and leave off your bad Latin'.

9 April 1999: On this day *The Times* reported that Beatrice, a mallard duck, had laid her eggs in the Cross Bath, which was part of the new Spa project. Together with Arthur, her mate, she successfully held up the work until a solution could be found.

14 April 1967: A lorry carrying 18 tons of peat ran into the wall of Twerton Infants' School during the night. There were no casualties, and lessons continued as normal the following day.

17 April 1960: On this day the 21-year-old American musician Edward Raymond ('Eddie') Cochran died at St Martin's Hospital, Bath. The previous day he had been involved in a serious car accident on the A4 at Chippenham whilst on a UK tour. The taxi in which he was travelling blew a tyre and crashed into a lamppost. A plaque marks the spot, and there is also a memorial stone in the grounds of the hospital.

18 April 1862: The Theatre Royal in Beauford Square was destroyed by fire, the cause of which was never discovered. The building had been insured for a mere £4,000 – a totally inadequate sum. A company was formed to rebuild on the old site, and the new theatre was opened the following year.

24 April 1990: Over 100 shops were closed by their owners in a protest against the introduction of a new uniform business rate. The protest took the form of a mock funeral with a hearse and 'mourners'.

25 April 1942: At 11 p.m. on this day (a Saturday) occurred the first of the German Luftwaffe's 'Baedeker' air raids on the city, which continued over the next two days. High explosives and incendiary bombs were dropped and the streets were raked with machine-gun fire. 417 people were killed and over 1,000 injured. More than 1,900 buildings were affected, of which over 1,000 were seriously damaged or destroyed.

26 April 1764: The Revd George Austen and Cassandra Leigh were married at the church of St Swithin, Walcot. They subsequently had eight children, of whom the novelist Jane is the most famous.

2 May 1844: William Beckford, novelist, art collector and eccentric, died at his home in Lansdown Crescent on this day. Known as 'England's wealthiest son', he was reputedly the richest commoner in England. He built the tower which is named after him on Lansdown Hill and is interred in a granite sarcophagus nearby.

8 May 1923: This was the day on which the legendary English cricketer Jack Hobbs made his hundredth first-class century, in a game between Surrey and Somerset which was played in Bath. He would go on to make a further 99 'tons', an unequalled record.

10 May 1910: Huge crowds gathered outside the Guildhall and the surrounding streets for the proclamation of King George V. High Street was completely blocked, with people standing on the upper decks of dangerously overcrowded buses.

11 May 973: On this day, according to the *Anglo-Saxon Chronicle,* the coronation of the Saxon King Edgar took place in the then Bath Abbey, on the festival of Whitsun. Edgar had become King of a united England on the death of his brother in 959, but his coronation did not take place until he reached the thirtieth year of his age.

12 May 1660: Bath became the first city to proclaim the accession of Charles II as King after his return from exile and the restoration of the monarchy.

14 May 2011: This day saw the reopening of the Holburne Museum after a three-year, £11.2 million restoration and development project, which included the building of a glass and ceramic extension at the rear.

17 May 1755: This day saw the first full performance in Bath of George Frideric Handel's oratorio *Messiah*. The venue was Wiltshire's Assembly Rooms on Terrace Walk.

18 May 1742: The Royal Mineral Water Hospital opened its doors to the first patients. It was then called the Bath General

Infirmary, but it underwent a change of name in the 1830s. It was the first purpose-built hospital in Bath.

19 May 1767: The foundation stone of the first house in John Wood the Younger's Royal Crescent was laid on this day. The project would take nearly eight years to complete and is regarded as the crowning glory of Bath's Georgian architecture.

21 May 1782: This day saw the last appearance on a Bath stage of the celebrated actress Sarah Siddons. The occasion was a benefit performance of the tragedy *The Distresed Mother* by Jean Racine.

23 May 1754: On this day the architect John Wood the Elder was born in Bath. His family moved to London, where he became a joiner in Soho. Returning to Bath in 1725, he was responsible for designing some of its most famous architecture, including the Parades, Queen Square and The Circus.

29 May 1752: The foundation stone of the new King Edward VI Grammar School in Broad Street was laid by Francis Hailes, Mayor of Bath. The school had been founded in 1552, using funds from the Dissolution of the Monasteries.

30 May 1797: The abolitionist William Wilberforce and Barbara Ann Spooner were married at St Swithin's church, Walcot. She was a lineal descendant of Cecily Neville, mother of Richard III.

1 June 1971: On this day Bath City Council issued an order requiring Miss Wellesley-Colley, of No. 22 Royal Crescent, to restore her front door to its original colour, after she had painted it primrose yellow. Her refusal led to a High Court action.

6 June 1877: The 'Halfpenny' Bridge, crossing the Avon at Widcombe, near the railway station, collapsed under the weight of people queuing to pay their tolls, killing at least ten people and injuring more than fifty.

9 June 1780: A 'most alarming riot' took place in Bath, which began with a footman and some boys breaking the windows of a Catholic priest's house. A mob soon gathered and the Riot Act was read by the mayor. Eventually, after several buildings had been burned, the rioters were persuaded to disperse. This riot was part of a series of anti-Catholic disturbances which mostly took place in London, and became known as the 'Gordon' Riots, after the president of the Protestant Association of London, Lord George Gordon.

12 June 1668: The famous diarist Samuel Pepys arrived with his family in Bath, and, being too weary from the journey to eat, went to bed without any supper.

20 June 1970: No. 1 Royal Crescent was officially opened to the public as an eighteenth-century domestic museum. It had been bought in 1967 by shipping millionaire Bernard Cayzer (1914–81), who presented the house to Bath Preservation Trust for restoration.

29 June 1764: This day saw the death of Ralph Allen, philanthropist and entrepreneur, at his home at Prior Park. Cornish by birth, he came to Bath in 1710, where he first became Postmaster and then owner of the stone mines at Combe Down. He built his mansion overlooking Bath and was a great benefactor to the city and was elected mayor in 1742. He is buried in the churchyard at Claverton on the outskirts of Bath.

5 July 1643: The Battle of Lansdown, an early engagement of the English Civil War (1642–51), took place on this day. The forces of King and Parliament clashed, with the Parliamentarians holding the high ground and the Royalists attacking uphill, in the course of which they suffered heavy casualties. The Parliamentary soldiers managed to slip away under cover of darkness.

6 July 1738: The foundation stone of Bath's General Hospital (later to become the Mineral Water Hospital) was laid.

7 July 1965: Former England Rugby player Jeremy Guscott was born in Bath. He began his career playing for Bath and went on to play for England and for the British and Irish Lions. He currently works full-time for the BBC.

8 July 1815: The acclaimed Shakespearean actor Edmund Kean appeared on the stage of the Theatre Royal in *The Merchant of Venice*, playing the role of Shylock. He was only 27 at the time.

10 July 1968: Torrential rainfall led to severe flooding in the West Country, with Bath suffering particularly badly. 5½in (about 14cm) of rain fell in the space of 24 hours, and many homes and businesses were devastated.

18 July 1996: The gardens of Prior Park opened to the public after a £650,000 restoration by the National Trust. The 28-acre gardens, which were part of Ralph Allen's estate, are among the finest in the country. Part of the work was carried out by 'Capability' Brown in the eighteenth century.

19 July 1909: This day saw the opening of the Bath Pageant, a five-day festival celebrating the history of the city from earliest times in a series of tableaux involving over 3,000 performers. It was held in Royal Victoria Park

20 July 1929: Large numbers of people, including 1,000 Bath schoolchildren, gathered to celebrate the freeing of Cleveland Bridge from toll charges. The ceremony was performed by the Marquess of Bath. Cleveland was the last bridge in the city to become exempt from such charges.

23 July 2002: The actor Leo McKern died on this day at a nursing home near Bath and was cremated at Haycombe Cemetery. Born in Australia, he became famous in Britain as a stage, screen, television and radio actor. He is probably best remembered for his portrayal of Horace Rumpole in the television series *Rumpole of the Bailey*, written by John Mortimer.

31 July 2007: An unexploded Second World War bomb was discovered near Widcombe Infants' School and the area was cordoned off by police for 2 hours. The device was safely removed by a bomb disposal squad.

2 August 1784: On the evening of this day, the very first mail coach passed through Bath on its way to London, having started its journey in Bristol at 4 p.m. It arrived in London at 8 a.m. the next day – a journey of just 16 hours, which had previously taken anything up to 38.

3 August 1805: Christopher Anstey, poet and author of the satirical bestseller *The New Bath Guide* died at his home in the Royal Crescent. He is buried at St Swithin's, Walcot, and has a memorial tablet in Poets' Corner, Westminster Abbey.

5 August 2005: On this day, the former Bath College of Higher Education (which had been renamed Bath Spa University College) was granted full university status by the Privy Council, becoming Bath Spa University.

7 August 2003: On the evening of this day, The Three Tenors (Luciano Pavarotti, Placido Domingo and José Carreras) performed together for the last time in an open-air concert on the lawns in front of the Royal Crescent. This was part of a celebration to mark the opening of the new, multi-million-pound Thermae Bath Spa. Unfortunately, a series of delays meant that the Spa did not open for another three years.

8 August 1799: Jane Austen's aunt, Mrs Leigh Perrot, was charged with the theft of lace from a Bath shop. Committed for trial at Taunton Assizes, she was subsequently acquitted when the charge was proved to be false.

16 August 1991: Fire gutted the interior of Prior Park Mansion. The fire, which was probably caused by an electrical fault, started on the top floor and spread downwards. Restoration work took three years.

19 August 1808: Joseph Lockier, a Bath resident, was struck by lightning in Farley Wood, and apparently 'remained alive with no sustenance but grass' until 8 September.

24 August 1865: The Royal School, for the daughters of army officers, opened on Lansdown. Founded as a result of the Crimean War, it was initially open only to Protestant families.

29 August 1827: Major Charles Edward Davis, architect and antiquary, was born near Bath on this day. He was responsible for the rediscovery and redevelopment of the Roman Baths in 1869 and was appointed City Architect and Surveyor to the Corporation of Bath.

31 August 1814: Admiral Arthur Phillip RN, formerly first Governor of New South Wales, Australia, died at his house in Bennett Street, when, according to some accounts, he fell from an upstairs window. He had retired to Bath at the age of 67, and had been suffering from declining health for some time.

1 September 1318: This day saw the signing and witnessing of a charter granting the Bishop of Bath and Wells the right to an annual fair, to be held in Bath on the feast day of St Peter and St Paul (29 June).

4 September 1590: This was the day on which Queen Elizabeth I granted a Royal Charter to the city of Bath. Among its provisions were the right for Bath to be called 'a city of itself', the definition of the city's boundaries, the right to establish a prison and the mayor to be chosen yearly 'on the Monday before the feast of St Michael', or Michaelmas (29 September).

7 September 1802: This day saw the first manned ascent from Bath of a hot-air balloon. It took place in Sydney Gardens, and the pilot was a Frenchman, André Jacques Garnerin, who was already a noted pioneer of balloon flight.

8 September 1891: Henry ('Harry') Dainton, a Bath stonemason, was arrested for the murder of his wife, Hannah, whose body had been discovered in the river Avon. Dainton was subsequently convicted of her murder, and on 15 December he was hanged at Shepton Mallet Gaol.

12 September 2014: For the first time, Bath played host to the Tour of Britain cycle race. Stage Six of the race started from Royal Avenue and continued via the edge of Salisbury Plain, to finish at Hemel Hempstead.

13 September 2014: The British Beard and Moustache Championships were held at the Bath Pavilion and were a sell-out success. The event was founded in 2012 and raises large sums for charities such as Macmillan Cancer Support.

23 September 2008: An explosion rocked the centre of Bath when a gas canister blew up on the construction site for the SouthGate shopping centre. Two nearby streets were evacuated, but fortunately there were no casualties.

29 September 2015: This day marked the official opening of the Gainsborough Bath Spa Hotel in Beau Street. The hotel, which is owned by the Malaysian YTL Corporation, is the only hotel in the UK to contain a naturally heated thermal spa.

30 September 1771: The Upper Assembly Rooms in Bennett Street opened with a *ridotto*, a combined dance and concert. The rooms were designed by the younger John Wood and the final cost of building amounted to £20,000.

1 October 2003: On this day Bath Tourism Plus was launched. This is the destination marketing organisation for the city, and took over the management of tourism promotion from Bath and North East Somerset Council.

4 October 1947: Former Conservative Member of Parliament Ann Noreen Widdecombe was born in Bath on this day. She attended Oxford University and was elected to the House of Commons in 1987, where she became known for her forthright views, particularly on foxhunting and abortion. She has written several books, both fiction and non-fiction, and retired from politics in 2010.

7 October 1873: The clergyman and diarist Francis Kilvert attended the Church Congress Service in Bath Abbey, where the Bishop of Derry 'preached an admirable sermon nearly an hour long'.

12 October 1805: This day saw the opening of the new Theatre Royal in Beauford Square with a performance of Shakespeare's *Richard III,* which promised the theatregoers 'new Scenery, Dresses, Machinery and other Decorations'. The previous theatre in Old Orchard Street became a Roman Catholic chapel and then a Masonic Lodge.

16 October 1831: Rioters attacked the White Hart Inn in Stall Street, where a troop of Yeomanry cavalry were gathering prior to leaving for Bristol to help in quelling the rioting taking place there. They were repelled by soldiers wielding red-hot pokers.

17 October 1922: On this day, the celebrated actor Dame Ellen Terry unveiled a plaque to another great Shakespearean performer, Mrs Sarah Siddons. The plaque is located on the wall of No. 33 The Paragon, where Mrs Siddons lived for several years.

18 October 1897: This day saw the laying of the foundation stone for the Victoria Art Gallery in Bridge Street. It was named in honour of Queen Victoria's Diamond Jubilee, marking her sixty years on the throne.

On the evening of the same day in 1938, the Assembly Rooms were reopened with a Gala Ball after a £30,000 restoration. Four years later the interior would be destroyed by incendiary bombs.

23 October 1894: Bath experienced 'The Great Flood', when the Avon burst its banks and much of the lower part of the city was inundated.

25 October 2015: The first Bristol to Bath Marathon was held, the first inter-city marathon to be run in the UK. More than 6,000 runners competed in the 26.2-mile (42km) event between the two cities, with women making up one-third of the entry. The winner finished with a time of 2 hours 31 minutes.

27 October 1750: The new theatre in Old Orchard Street (then known as the St James' Theatre) opened with a performance of Shakespeare's *Henry IV, Part Two*. In 1768 it was granted a royal patent and became the Theatre Royal, the first playhouse outside London to be so designated.

28 October 1830: This was the day on which the 11-year-old Princess Victoria visited the city, accompanied by her mother, the Duchess of Kent. Whilst here, the princess officially opened the Royal Victoria Park. She would ascend the throne seven years later.

This same date, in 1852, saw the official opening of Kingswood School, on the northern slopes of the city.

3 November 2014: The legendary jazz clarinettist Bernard Stanley 'Acker' Bilk died at Bath's Royal United Hospital at the age of 85.

4 November 2009: This day saw the opening of Phase One of the SouthGate shopping centre in the south of the city. Phases Two and Three opened in May and August the following year. This development replaced the previous shops from the 1960s and 1970s.

13 November 2014: Two cygnets landed in a Bath cemetery and began wandering across adjacent roads, causing chaos. They were eventually captured by two police community support officers and released on the nearby canal. This incident is curiously reminiscent of a scene from the 2007 film *Hot Fuzz*.

16 November 2007: During archaeological excavations on the site of the new Gainsborough Hotel, a hoard of over 17,500 Roman coins was discovered. The Beau Street Hoard, as it is known, is the fifth largest so far found in Britain, and has initially been valued at £150,000.

18 November 1778: On this day Jean Baptisite, Vicomte du Barré, was killed in a duel on Bathampton Down. His opponent was Captain Rice, with whom he had quarrelled over sharing the winnings from a card game in the Royal Crescent.

19 November 1790: The Arctic explorer and navigator Sir William Parry was born in Bath on this day. He made five expeditions to the Arctic between 1818 and 1827 and later became Governor of Greenwich Hospital, London.

20 November 1929: A freight train hauling thirty-three empty coal trucks from Evercreech to Bath was derailed at the entrance to Bath goods yard. The driver and two railway employees were killed and the fireman and guard were badly injured. An enquiry concluded that the crew had been overcome by smoke and fumes while the train was going through Combe Down Tunnel.

3 December 1976: This day saw the closure of the Hot Bath Treatment Centre, due to the Mineral Water Hospital no longer using the facility because they had built their own pool in the hospital. National Health Service patients from the 'Min' had previously made up about 95 per cent of its clientele.

7 December 1189: Bath got its first charter, granted by Richard I. It encouraged trading by granting freedom from tolls and was the first step towards self-government in the city.

8 December 1899: The foundation stone for the Empire Hotel in Orange Grove was laid by the Mayor of Bath, R.E. Dickinson, MP. The building was completed in 1901 and is now apartments and restaurants.

9 December 1974: A 5lb bomb exploded near the centre of Bath, causing substantial damage to the Georgian shopping arcade known as The Corridor. A warning had been given, and fortunately there were no injuries. The IRA afterwards claimed responsibility.

10 December 1728: Work was begun on the foundations for the first houses of John Wood the Elder's Queen Square. The square would take almost eight years to complete and would become the first fashionable area in the Georgian city.

11 December 1987: Bath was officially inscribed on the UNESCO list of World Heritage Sites because of its architectural, cultural and historical importance.

15 December 1914: George Joseph Smith, the 'Brides in the Bath' murderer, married his last victim, Margaret Lofty, at No. 3 North Parade. At that time the building was the Bath Register Office.

16 December 1920: The former Electric Theatre (1910) in Westgate Street reopened on this day as the Beau Nash Cinema. This eventually closed in 2005 and has since been renovated and reopened as the Komedia Comedy Club.

17 December 1945: On this day the author Jacqueline Wilson (*née* Aitken) was born in Bath. After writing several crime novels she dedicated herself to children's books, several of which have been adapted for theatre and television. She is now one of Britain's best-selling authors, and was created a Dame in 2008.

21 December 1820: The Lower Assembly Rooms, which stood on the east side of Terrace Walk overlooking Parade Gardens, were largely destroyed by a fire on this day. They were rebuilt as the Bath Royal Literary and Scientific Institution, but were finally demolished in 1933.

23 December 1834: Thomas Robert Malthus, clergyman, scholar and author of the highly influential *Essay on the Principle of Population*, died at St Catherine, near Bath. He is buried in the abbey, where he has a monument.

24 December 1880: This day saw the official opening of the Bath Tramway Company, with its first horse-drawn tram travelling over the newly laid line. The service operated until 1902, when it was taken over and electrified.

25 December 1191: This day saw the death of Reginald FitzJocelin (*c*. 1140–91), former Bishop of Bath and Wells and founder of Bath's St John's Hospital. He was elected Archbishop of Canterbury, but chose to become a monk at Bath Abbey instead, and died there only a month later. He is buried close to the high altar of the abbey.

31 December 1724: The newly appointed 'proprietors' of the project to make the Avon navigable between Bath and Bristol met for the first time in Bath. They included the entrepreneur and stone-mine owner Ralph Allen and Bath architect Thomas Attwood. The project was completed three years later.

BIBLIOGRAPHY

Amphlett, D.G., *The Bath Book of Days* (The History Press, 2014) – A really useful and well-researched source for notable dates in the history of the city.

Cunliffe, Barry, *Roman Bath Discovered* (Tempus, 2000) – Authoritative guide to the Roman town.

Eglin, John, *The Imaginary Autorcrat; Beau Nash and the invention of Bath* (Profile Books, 2005) – A modern biography of the 'King of Bath'.

Elliott, Kirsten, *A Window on Bath* (Millstream Books, Bath, 1994) – Things to look out for while exploring the city.

Fawcett, Trevor (compiler), *Voices of Eighteenth-century Bath* (Ruton, 1995) – Material from original eighteenth-century sources.

Forsyth, Michael, *Bath (Pevsner Architectural Guides)* (Yale University Press, 2003) – Invaluable guide to Bath's architecture.

Freeman, Jean, *Jane Austen in Bath* (The Jane Austen Society, 2002) – Life and times of the great novelist.

Gadd, David, *Georgian Summer* (Countryside Books, 1987) – Very readable guide to social life in the city.

Goldsmith, Oliver (Collected works), Life of Richard Nash, Esquire (Macmillan and Co., 1878) – The life of Nash by one who knew him.

Haddon, John, *Bath* (B.T. Batsford Ltd, 1973) – Excellent general history of the city.

Hamilton, Meg, *Bath Before Beau Nash* (Kingsmead Press, Bath, 1978) – Well-researched guide to pre-Georgian Bath.

Hinde, Thomas, *Tales from the Pump Room* (Victor Gollancz Ltd, 1988) – Gossip, scandal and anecdotes of life in the city.

Hopkins-Clarke, M., *A Struggle to Survive; The Theatre Royal 1805-1905* (Self-published, printed by MLD Bath) – Very detailed and informative account of the first 100 years of the Theatre.

Ison, Walter, *The Georgian Buildings of Bath* (Kingsmead Press, Bath, 1980) – Very comprehensive information about the building of the eighteenth-century city.

Lane, Maggie, *A Charming Place* (Millstream Books, 1988) – Very readable picture of the Bath that Jane Austem knew.

Lascelles, Frank, *The Story of the Bath Pageant* (Edward Everard, Bristol, 1909) – The official account of the Bath Historical Pageant of 1909.

Lowndes, William, *The Royal Crescent in Bath* (Redcliffe Press, Bristol, 1981) – The story of Bath's premier address and its most notable inhabitants.

Lowndes, William, *The Theatre Royal at Bath* (Redcliffe Press, Bristol, 1982) – The development of the theatre from its eighteenth-century beginnings.

Mowl, Tim, *John Wood; Architect of Obsessio* (Millstream Books, 1988) – A very comprehensive account of the man and his works.

Raffael, Michael, *Bath Curiosities* (Birlinn, 2006) – Unusual and intriguing aspects of Bath

Rothnie, Niall, *Unknown Bath* (Ashgrove Press, Bath, 1986) – Curious stories and facts that bring Bath's history to life.

Sitwell, Edith, *Bath* (Redcliffe Press, Bristol, 1983) – The great writer's own take on the history and people of the city.

Smith, R.A.L., *Bath* (B.T. Batsford Ltd, 1945) – A good general history written from an early twentieth-century perspective.

Stace, Bernard, *Bath Abbey Monuments* (Millstream Books, 1993) – A useful little booklet detailing some of the more important memorials in the Abbey.

Tames, Richard & Sheila, *A Traveller's History of Bath* (Arris Publishing Ltd, 2009) – Wide-ranging look at the history of the city in all its aspects.

White, Diana, *Stories of Bath* (Millstream Books, 2006) – Well-written collection, containing some less well-known stories about the city.

Also archive material from the *Bath Chronicle* and its predecessors, the *Bath Herald* and *Bath Journal*.